DIY
Woven Art

DIY Woven Art

Inspiration and Instruction for Handmade
Wall Hangings, Rugs, Pillows, and More!

Rachel Denbow

INTERWEAVE.
interweave.com

Contents

Introduction

If you're anything like me, you're naturally drawn to items that seem to carry a story with them. In their lines and colors, they share information about the hands that shaped them and capture an image of a specific season; they are created with intention and purpose, even if only to offer their beauty.

Historically, handwoven textiles have incorporated motifs that share cultural mores and use colors indicative of the resources available in their region. This absolutely reflects my first weaving experience as a fourth-grade girl who was eager to earn a merit badge by finishing a pot holder. I may have spent only thirty minutes constructing a wonky square made from cheap fabric bands on a plastic loom, but that pot holder represented so much more. It was proof of life in a sort of coming-of-age story. I wasn't concerned with even edges or whether the rest of my troop would like my design; I just knew I really liked figuring out how to turn a pile of fabric bands into something else altogether.

As a grown woman with years of creative ventures under my belt, I'm still completely smitten with exploring all the ways I can manipulate fibers to produce on-trend pieces that are aesthetically pleasing and, sometimes, completely practical. I have been able to create one-of-a-kind rugs from repurposed sheets, have given chairs new life using neon paracord, and have added so much color and texture to the walls of our home with each new wall hanging. Not only has weaving become an avenue of creative experimentation, it's been one of the easiest ways to quiet my mind at the end of a long day. My hands get busy, life slows down, and I'm able to find that peaceful place that leaves me more connected to myself and somehow to all the makers that have ever sat down at a loom.

As a new tribe of creative individuals continues to explore this ancient craft with new color stories and fresh eyes, it is my great pleasure to share some of the basic elements of frame-loom weaving. Included in this book are three different inexpensive ways to make your own looms as well as an overview of different types of fibers you might use based on your woven project. I share my design process as I sketch shapes and choose colors for each new piece and fill you in on how to avoid that dreaded hourglass shape. I also provide a selection of techniques for you to use as you discover your own unique weaving style.

If you're absolutely new to weaving, this project-based book will take you step by step through a few simple wall hangings to help you wrap your head around the basic process. Then each new project covers new steps and techniques. All you need to bring to the table is your enthusiasm (and a little patience), and you'll end up with a piece you'll actually want to hang in your own space. If you have been playing with warp and weft for years, it's my hope this book inspires you to test your comfort zone and look for ways to reinvent the familiar things. Whether it's incorporating an idea from another medium, such as embroidery or quilting, or subscribing to a new color story pulled straight from a home décor blog, there are always opportunities to expand our current creative boundaries.

The best part about learning this medium is that you are joining a growing number of makers who have already set up their looms and are learning as they go. There are so many talented fiber artists teaching what they know and encouraging community through their social media platforms and pop-up workshops around the world. We've come a long way from pot holders, friend! I'm so excited and honored to be on this weaving journey with you.

—Rachel

Chapter One

Materials

Frame-loom weaving is one of the more user-friendly mediums to explore because you don't need a lot of equipment to get started. My first woven wall hanging was made by nailing two rows of nails into the back of a salvaged cabinet drawer! I used inexpensive yarn from a thrift store and used my fingers to weave my design. Once I realized I had found my new favorite medium, I began to educate myself on the tools and materials available to frame-loom weaving so I could decide what was necessary for the next level of weaving I wanted to attempt. This chapter is a simple overview of the types of frame looms, yarns, and tools you may want to use in your weaving adventure.

Simple Looms

All of the projects in this book will be made from one of three kinds of looms: a cardboard loom, a lap-sized frame loom, or an oversize standing frame loom. These are the most basic types of looms, but you can use them to produce beautiful flat-weave tapestries, wall hangings with tons of texture, and pieces that can be turned into utilitarian items such as a pillow, a clutch, or a rug.

The most basic looms consist of either a solid shape, such as a thick piece of cardboard, or a frame shape, with negative space in the center for easy access to the back of your woven piece. Some frame looms will have either notches or pegs along the top and bottom for your warp (the fiber that acts as the foundation of your woven piece). The weft is then woven horizontally across the warp on the front side of the loom.

You can also use a square or rectangle shape without notches and pegs, such as an actual picture frame, where your warp will wrap vertically over the top and bottom of the frame. This kind of warp will require twining, or the use of a tool such as a ruler or dowel, to help the warp threads come together again after they've been separated by the top and bottom of the frame. Don't worry if none of that makes sense yet. I'll be sharing visuals for warping both kinds of frame looms, so you can decide which type best suits you.

With so many types of looms, how does one even choose where to start? Most of the looms you'll use are chosen based on the type of project you want to make.

From front to back: Cardboard loom, adjustable frame loom, mini handmade loom on scrap wood, large handmade loom on scrap wood, oversize frame loom.

Cardboard Looms

If you're interested in making a sampler while you work out the kinks, you might want to start with a smaller cardboard loom. Cardboard looms can be taken anywhere, help you experiment with warp and weft color before diving into a larger project, and are easy to customize depending on the size of your project. Plus, they won't cost you a thing if you decide to reuse a flap of the cardboard box from your latest online order. Just be sure your cardboard is thick, like a box you'd send in the mail, and not like the cardboard from your favorite cereal box. If it bends too easily, your warp will lose its tension, and you'll have a hot mess on your hands. Smaller weavings on a cardboard loom can easily be pulled out while you're waiting for your morning train, when you're in between classes, or when you're waiting to meet a friend for coffee.

Lap-Sized Frame Looms

Frame looms with pegs or notches across the top and bottom come in a range of sizes and price points. You can find them in a variety of Etsy shops by themselves, but many are sold with a set of weaving tools and even starter bundles of yarn. You can also follow the instructions in this book to build your own with a few simple tools. No matter your budget or level of commitment, you can acquire a loom to suit your specific needs.

Frame-loom weaving is my default method for most of my woven projects. It allows for a sturdier tension than a cardboard loom as well as a more pleasing design due to even and consistent spacing. You don't have to worry about your warp bending your frame out of shape, and you can work with heavier materials such as wool roving and fabric strips. I also love the ability to easily weave over and under without having to lift my warp off of the cardboard with my tapestry needle or fingers as I weave each row. You can add fringe to the bottom to add length and texture to your wall hangings or fill the entire frame with weft for a piece that can be sewn into a pillow or placemat.

These types of looms are portable and easy to store, although they're usually not as easy to throw in your purse and go. They can be used perched on a table or in your lap, depending on its construction. You can also find standing tabletop frame looms that have an adjustable or removable base at the bottom for easy transport.

Oversize Standing Frame Looms

An oversize standing frame loom will be the best option for larger projects such as a statement wall hanging, oversize pillow shams, or any type of rug. You can purchase them or make your own with a quick trip to the hardware store. They do take up more space than a lap loom, so you'll want to be sure you have room to keep it set up for awhile, as projects of this size will usually require a few sessions to complete. The good news is, they can easily come apart for transport if you move, and many can be stored flat under your bed or in a closet.

These three looms are just the tip of the iceberg when it comes to the variety available. Other looms range from a rigid-heddle loom (a next-level loom with more intricate parts and a more complicated setup) to a multiple-shaft floor loom, perfect for making fabric as well as intricately designed shawls, throws, and even rugs. Let's not get ahead of ourselves, though! Each of the looms used in this book will allow you to create beautiful projects you can be proud of while learning techniques that will provide the necessary framework for your creative exploration.

Tools and Accessories

An artist may only be as good as his/her tools, but there's something to be said for working your way up from a sensible starting point. Below are some of the most basic frame-loom weaving tools that will make your work more enjoyable and that can be found at a variety of price points to fit your budget.

Weaving or Tapestry Needles: These come in a variety of lengths and widths ranging 2½"–8" (6.5–20.5cm) long and can be made of wood, metal, plastic, or acrylic. The eye of the needle is usually wide enough for a variety of yarn sizes to be used, and these needles can be found in most fiber art shops or online.

Shed Stick: This is a long rectangular piece that looks like a ruler and may or may not have smooth ends. It is woven over and under across your warp to separate every other warp thread and then angled perpendicular to the warp to create a shed for your weaving shuttle to easily slide through in one direction. Using the shed stick helps save a lot of time when working on large blocks of color across your woven piece. It can also be used to help regulate tension when pushed firmly to the top of the loom. You can easily use a ruler or yardstick as a substitute.

Stick Shuttles: These are usually rectangular or canoe shaped with notches at each end. They are wrapped with fiber and slide across your weaving through the space made between your warp when you use a shed stick. They are more efficient than using a tapestry needle when you're weaving wide blocks of the same fiber or are weaving rows because you can use longer lengths of yarn.

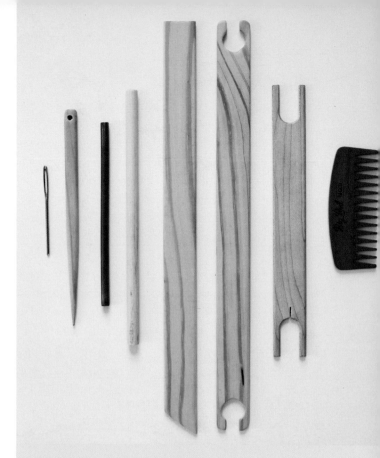

From left to right: 3" (7.5 cm) tapestry needle, 7" (18 cm) tapestry needle, copper pipe, wooden dowel, 12" (30.5 cm) shed stick, 12" stick shuttle, 8" (20.5 cm) stick shuttle, weaving comb.

Weaving Combs: These can come in a variety of widths and are used to help press down each new weft row evenly as you go. There are a variety of beautiful wooden and acrylic combs on the market, but you can use your fingers, a fork, or a hair comb from the drugstore as well.

Rods and Hangers: If you're creating a wall hanging, you'll need something sturdy to hang it from. You can use wooden dowel rods from the craft store, copper piping cut to size from the hardware store, acrylic rods, driftwood, or sticks found in nature.

Yarn

While you may initially want to choose fibers for your woven pieces based on their specific color and texture, I find that the more I learn about the qualities of each kind of yarn, the better I can use it. It has helped me avoid ordering the wrong kind of yarn online on more than one occasion as well!

When weaving on a frame loom, you can choose from 100% natural fibers such as cotton, hemp, jute, linen, wool, alpaca, silk, etc., or you can incorporate synthetic fibers such as acrylic and polyester blends. Different kinds of yarns will have different thicknesses and textures. While it's incredibly helpful to know which yarn is more appropriate for knitting a thin cardigan compared to a thick pair of woolen socks, you'll want to focus more on the amount of space per row each fiber takes up as well as how its texture will look when paired with other fibers to create an interesting piece.

Yarn Fibers

I'm of the opinion that starting with synthetic fibers is a great way to decide if you're going to enjoy this medium without investing a lot of money up front. But in the end, my most favorite woven pieces have been made from natural fibers. You try holding onto a skein of 100% merino wool and then walking away. It's just so dang soft! You'll soon learn what you like best, and then you'll inevitably wind up with what is commonly known as your yarnicorn, the fiber you love so much you keep it tucked away until the perfect project comes along.

Each specific fiber offers its own unique qualities to a woven design depending on how it's spun. The fiber can be offered in its purest form or blended together. The list below is not comprehensive, by any means, but includes the yarns you're most likely to use.

100% Cotton: Used for warp as well as weft, this type of plant-based fiber is strong and creates a lot of texture when used as a fringe or woven into your wall hanging. It's a little stiffer than wool, alpaca, or silk but is also less expensive.

Synthetic: Synthetic fibers, including nylon, acrylic, and polyester, are commercially produced and sometimes blended with other fibers such as wool. It is usually a fraction of the cost of natural fiber yarn but can also have a shiny look to it.

From top: Poly/wool blend, 100% wool, cotton, alpaca/wool blend, llama/wool/silk blend, 100% wool.

Wool: This is a natural animal-based fiber that is commonly used in woven pieces. It is easy to work with and offers a variety of textures depending on the type and quality of the wool. Wool roving is the stretched-out, cotton-candy-looking fiber that has yet to be spun into yarn.

Alpaca: Alpaca is similar to sheep's wool but is hypoallergenic. It has a lovely softness to it.

Silk: This is a delicate but strong fiber with a bit of shine.

Bamboo: This plant-based fiber is great for weaving since you'll likely not wash your woven project often, if ever. Bamboo yarn tends to need handwashing and air-drying or dry cleaning to avoid shrinkage or heat damage. It's strong, soft, sustainable, and has antibacterial properties. Bamboo is often blended with other fibers such as wool and silk.

I prefer using a cotton yarn for my warps because of its durability, but you'll find yourself wanting to experiment with different fibers and colors in order to create varied designs. Start with cotton yarn and then branch out once you become familiar with it. You can find cones of inexpensive cotton yarn at most hobby stores in off-white as well as a variety of colors.

Yarn Sizes

Fibers come in different thicknesses and weights and are classified as such to help users understand what kind of project they'd be best suited for. For example, wool can be spun into a fine laceweight yarn or a super chunky yarn. A laceweight yarn is much more delicate and thin, as it's been processed for projects that require less bulk. It's great for crafting doilies but not the best for a warm sweater. Likewise, chunky wool yarn is perfect for knitting a cozy throw blanket but wouldn't work so well if you wanted a fine pair of socks. Understanding the classification and weight of a yarn will help you choose the best thickness for the design you'd like to create, especially when you're working with a variety of yarns.

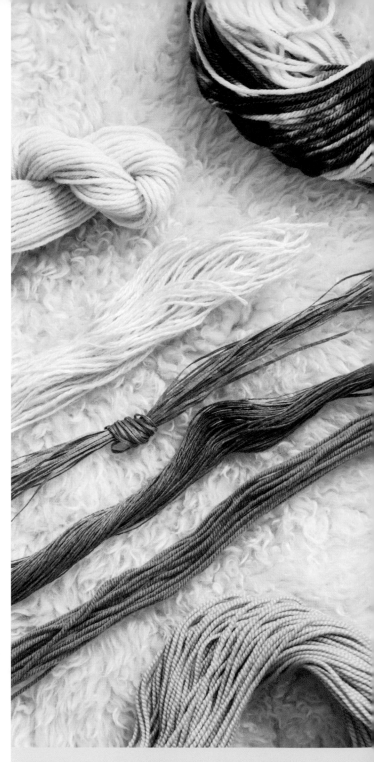

From top right: Hand-dyed wool, factory-dyed wool, 100% cotton, cotton gima, 100% linen, 100% wool, wool/silk blend.

Lace: A delicate yarn in terms of thickness, it's used to make lace and doilies. In regard to weaving, it would be a better choice for smaller projects such as woven necklaces.

Fingering: Usually designated for making socks, this type of yarn is light and would also be ideal for intricate details on a woven piece or a smaller project.

Sport: Used for lightweight clothing items, this yarn is a good option for weaving when you incorporate a design.

Light Worsted: This is an average thickness of yarn used for making scarves, blankets, and sweaters. This type of yarn is a great option for filling in large swaths of space as well as creating designs.

Worsted: A thicker yarn, it creates a lovely texture when paired with sport or light worsted yarns. Use it to create a substantial fringe at the bottom of your wall hangings or to create a textured but sturdy pillow top.

Bulky: This is the ultimate yarn for adding in texture and makes quick work since each row is substantially thicker than those made with other types of yarn.

Yarn Quantities

Determining yarn yardage when weaving a wall hanging is less clear-cut than when weaving a table runner on a rigid-heddle loom or even knitting a scarf. Less often are you re-creating a design than just experimenting with your own ideas and using the yarn already available to you to determine the outcome of the design. Elements that affect the yardage of yarn include the size and texture of your yarn, the amount of different yarns used in your design, the various stitches you incorporate, the length of your rya knots, and the dimensions of your loom.

To determine yardage for your warp, count how many pegs or notches you'll warp at the top of your frame loom and multiply that by 2 (20 pegs x 2 = 40). Then measure the length between the top and bottom of your frame loom and add 1" (12" + 1" = 13"). Multiply that amount by your

From top to bottom: Laceweight, sportweight, light worsted-weight, worsted-weight, bulky, fingering-weight yarns.

first amount to find out how many inches of yarn you'll need (13 × 40 = 520). Then divide that amount by 36 to determine how many yards that makes (520 ÷ 36 = 14.4). I always like to add a little extra just in case, so I would round that up to 15 yards (13.7 m).

To determine weft yardage for your plain-weave design, I've discovered it's helpful to understand how many wraps per inch you will get from the yarn you want to use. Listed below is the number of wraps per inch for the most common yarn types.

Wraps Per Inch (WPI)

Lace: 18 or more wpi

Fingering: 16 wpi

Sport and Light Worsted: 14 wpi

Worsted: 12 wpi

Bulky: 10 wpi

That inch represents 1" (2.5 cm) of space running up the side of your warp. Multiply that number by 2 to determine how many weft rows you'll get per inch of space.

Then multiply that number by the width of your weft rows to determine how many inches of yarn you'll need just to fill that inch of warp space on your loom.

Divide by 36 to convert your inches to yards; the result will be the number of yards you'll need per inch to fill your warp with that specific yarn.

To determine yardage when using rya knots to create fringe, estimate the length you'll want from your fringe and multiply by 2. Add 1" (2.5 cm) to compensate for the wraparound. Now multiply that number by the number of strands per rya knot you'd like to use. Then multiply that number by the number of rya knots total. Divide it by 36 to convert your inches into yards, and you'll have the correct amount of yarn for your rya knots.

If you have a pre-sketched design, you will likely end up with a more accurate calculation. If you over-estimate, you can enjoy using the leftovers on a future project. If you underestimate, see if you can substitute with something you already have available or just practice your patience while you wait to

Multiply your WPI (wraps per inch) by 2 to determine how many weft rows you'll get per inch of space.

Multiply your weft rows per inch of space by the width of your warp to determine how many inches of yarn is needed to fill 1" (2.5 cm) of space across your warp.

get your hands on more of the same yarn. Once you've made one or two wall hangings, you'll start to recognize how much yarn you'll need for the different elements of each design. Be sure to purchase enough yarn from the same dyelot to have a consistent color throughout your work.

More Yarn and Weaving Options

It's exciting to see the ever-increasing hand-dyed and even natural-dyed color options being offered by small fiber businesses online. You may also be on the lookout for vintage fibers in the craft section at local thrift shops or flea markets.

The fun doesn't have to stop with yarn, either, people. I recently finished a larger wall hanging that used cut strips of a gauzy swaddle blanket that I used when my son was a newborn. It provided plenty of texture paired with a cotton warp and is an interesting contrast to the more intricate woven pieces hanging next to it. I've also used jewelry wire for the warp instead of cotton yarn and have incorporated dyed duck feathers into one of the projects in this book (page 108). The point is, if it bends a little, you can probably weave with it.

A variety of hand-dyed worsted-weight wool skeins from Knit Stitch Yarn.

Unlabeled Yarn

If you have access to unlabeled yarn, slip your thumb under the yarn and see how many rows will neatly sit next to each other between the top knuckle and the tip of your thumb, as that is generally about 1" (2.5 cm) long.

Soumak Tip

Keep in mind that soumak stitches (page 84) will require you to triple the length of yarn used, as they double back when woven across your warp.

Chapter Two

Loom DIY

Before you start your first woven project, you need to figure out what you'll use as a loom. The beauty of weaving is that you can create your warp on anything with opposing and fixed points or planes. This means you can use a cardboard box, a slab of wood, a solid tree branch with a V-shape, or the most complex loom on the market. This principle gives you the freedom to customize the size and shape of your project so you can create a mini woven necklace or a 2½' × 6' (76 × 1.8 m) runner for your hallway. It also means you don't have to invest in a store-bought loom until you decide, as many of us have, that weaving is your new favorite creative outlet and that you're willing to start donating plasma to help support your yarn habit.

One of the benefits of learning to make your own looms is that you can use supplies you may already have on hand or can repurpose scrap materials. I used an 18" × 48" (45.5 × 122 cm) piece of scrap wood that I found on someone's curb to create a primitive standing loom. I merely nailed in one row of nails as evenly as I could manage near the top edge and then another row about 18" farther down. It allowed me to weave while standing and wearing my newborn wrapped across my chest. I'd gently sway back and forth to soothe him while regaining some time to do something for myself. It was a sanity saver for the both of us! Nine months later, I

used the bottom section of that same board to hammer nails in the shape of a Christmas stocking to try my hand at a nontraditional shape. The stockings turned out better than I'd hoped and were fully functional after being sewn together with two cuts of flannel. That experimental project clued me in to the fact that my design options were wide open as long as I worked within the confines of opposing points or planes.

This chapter shares step-by-step plans for making a small flat loom, an adjustable tabletop frame loom, and an oversize frame loom while also sharing tips on how to shop for a store-bought loom when you're ready. It seems there are more loom designs on the market now than ever before thanks to the ingenuity of craftsmen and women who have married centuries-old ideas with new technology. If you're not interested in creating your own loom or would rather support the efforts of a small business, there are a great range of designs and price points from which to choose.

Cardboard Looms

If you're looking for a loom that won't cost you a dime and is as portable as it is practical, a handmade cardboard loom is a great place to start. You can cut the top off of the last box that came in the mail or pick up a thick mailer envelope from your local post office, and you're halfway there. Make sure you're using something that can withstand a little pressure from opposite ends and won't fold in half if you turn out to be an enthusiastic weaver.

Supplies

thick or sturdy piece of cardboard, cut to size of your choice	ruler
	pencil
washi tape	scissors

Making a Cardboard Loom

1   Make a pen mark every ¼" (6 mm) across the top and bottom edges of your cardboard loom and then cut on those marks about ¼" deep. Marking your notches closer together might cause them to tear easily, while notches farther apart may leave you with a loosey-goosey weave. I placed washi tape along the top and bottom edges for easier visibility, but it's not necessary (Fig. 1).

2   Tape one end of your warp yarn to the back side of the cardboard loom nearer to one side. Wrap the yarn up and over to the front side of the loom making sure it slides into the first notch on the top edge. Continue wrapping it through the first notch on the bottom edge and around to the back side of the loom again. Repeat wrapping it so that the yarn slides into the second notch on the top edge and then the second notch on the bottom edge and around to the back side again until you've wrapped your yarn all the way to the other side. End your warp by taping a 6" (15 cm) tail to the back side (Fig. 2).

3   The tension on your loom shouldn't be so tight that it causes your cardboard to warp into a bow shape or so loose that it sits slack on the front. Adjust your tension as necessary by pulling out the slack or loosening things up before cutting your yarn and taping it to the back. You'll be weaving only on the front side of your loom (Fig. 3). When designing your woven piece, be sure to allow for about 1" (2.5 cm) of unusable space near the top, as it will get harder and harder to weave all the way up on a flat loom. Instructions for getting your woven piece off this kind of loom are shared on page 40 of the first project.

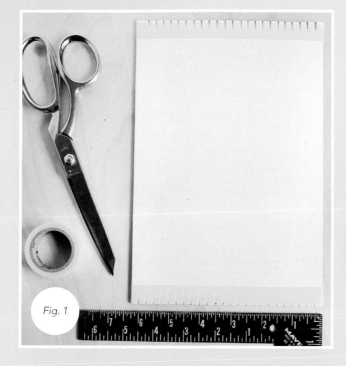

Fig. 1

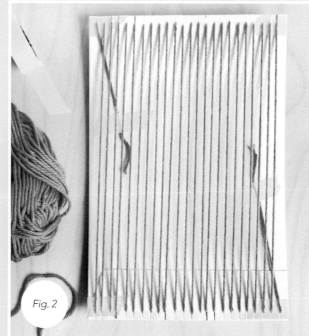

Fig. 2

Fig. 3

Adjustable Frame Looms

Creating your own adjustable frame loom isn't as hard as it sounds but will require access to a power drill. These instructions will allow you to make one loom that can create at least two different wall-hanging sizes. You can also remove the screws to disassemble your frame for transport or storage when not in use. If you don't have access to a power drill, you can easily simplify the instructions by hammering nails into the four corners in place of the screws for a fixed frame loom.

Supplies

4 cuts of poplar board 1" x 2" x 24" (2.5 x 5 x 61 cm) (actual size is ¾" x 1¼" x 24" [2 x 3.2 x 61 cm])	8 brass standard hex nuts, #8-32
	52 steel trim nails, 1½" (3.8 cm)
power drill	hammer
9/64 drill bit	handsaw
8 brass round-head slotted machine screws, #8-32 x 2	medium-grade sandpaper
	ruler
	pencil

Making an Adjustable Frame Loom

1   Cut 2 of your poplar boards down to 15" (38 cm) using your ruler, pencil, and handsaw. Sand down your rough edges as well as the surfaces of each piece of poplar. Place your 2 longer boards parallel to each other and about 15" (38 cm) apart. Then place your 2 shorter boards parallel to each other and resting on top of the longer boards so that they are flush in each corner and meet at 90-degree angles, creating a rectangle. Make 2 marks diagonal from each other in each corner. Be sure each mark is about ½" (1.3 cm) in from each edge so the holes you'll drill don't split the board. Predrill your holes using a 9/64 drill bit, making sure the edges of the corner are flush with each other. Add your screws and nuts to secure the top two corners (Fig. 1). Continue drilling the rest of the corners and add the rest of your screws.

2   To make your loom adjustable, use the bottom 15" (38 cm) board as your template and move it up as high as you'd like to create another set of holes on the longer boards. I made my second set of holes about 7" (18 cm) higher, but it's easily customizable to your specific needs. You can even add a third or fourth set of holes so long as the holes are at least 2" (5 cm) apart from each other to prevent the boards from splitting. Make sure all of your corner angles are at 90 degrees before marking and drilling (Fig. 2). Insert your screws and add the hex nuts to the back to secure.

3   Measure in 1¼" x ½" (3.2 x 1.3 cm) from the bottom right edge of the top board and then make a mark every ½" (1.3 cm) for a total of 26 marks. Repeat with the bottom board. The more consistently even you are with your marks, the better all of your woven wall hangings will look. You can remove your top and bottom boards to hammer your nails, or simply place one of your scraps of wood underneath the raised boards for support (Fig. 3). Carefully hammer your finishing nails into your marks about ½" so that they stick out about 1" (2.5 cm). Watch those fingers as you hammer away!

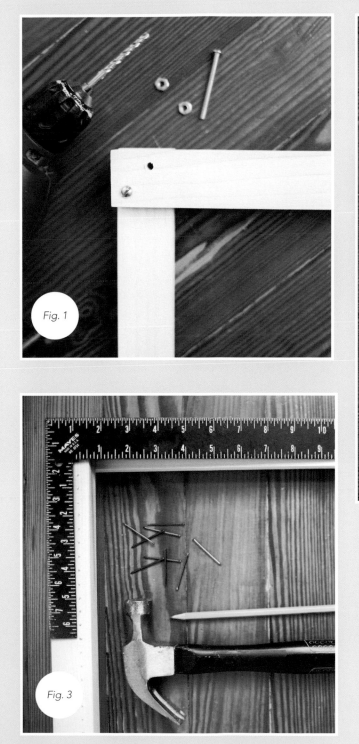

Fig. 1

Fig. 2

Fig. 3

Warping Your Adjustable Frame Loom

When you warped your cardboard loom, you wrapped your yarn in circles around the front and back because the cardboard notches aren't usually strong enough to hold your warp as you pull on it while weaving. Warping a wooden frame loom with nails, pegs, or notches on the top and bottom edges means you'll only be wrapping your warp yarn up and down the front side of your loom.

1   Tie a 1" (2.5 cm) loop knot in the loose end of your warp yarn and hook it over your first nail on the top board. I started a few nails in on mine so it would be easier to see on the loom. Wrap it down and around the corresponding nail on the bottom board and bring it back up to the second nail on the top board. Continue to zigzag up and down as you wrap your warp yarn across the front of your loom (Fig. 1). For an even number of warps, finish with another loop knot hooked to the last nail on the top board. If you end on the opposite board as you started, you'll have an odd number of warps. An even number is helpful when you are adding rya knots all the way across your wall hanging, as they need 2 warp threads per knot. An odd number is helpful when you need a center row for a symmetrical design.

2   Check your tension so that it's not too loose or too tight before you cut your warp yarn and tie your second loop knot. A loose tension will contribute to a messy piece, and a tension that is too tight will pull and make it hard to weave near the top. An inconsistently even tension will make it sloppy on one side.

One of the best ways to adjust tension is to pull on one end of the yarn and help it even out as it tightens across the nails. You can also weave a ¼" (6 mm) dowel rod or ruler through your warp and gently pull it toward the top of your loom. This will help evenly disperse some of the slack.

3   Cut a thick piece of cardboard that's at least 2" (5 cm) wider than the width of all of your warp threads and measures about 2.5" (6.5 cm) tall. Weave it over and under through your warp (Fig. 2) and pull it down to the bottom of the warp so it rests just above the nails (Fig. 3). This will act as a space holder for when you cut the woven wall hanging off the loom at the bottom and tie the warps in knots to keep your weft from falling out.

This step also allows for a cleaner finish at the top of your warps if you weave nearly to the top but then leave enough unusable room to insert your dowel or pipe. The dowel or pipe will keep your weft snugly in place, and you won't need to fuss with adding a hemstitch (page 50) or cutting your warps, tying them off, and stitching them into the back of your weaving.

You may want to bypass this step if you find that you enjoy weaving your design from the bottom up, as you'll naturally finish at the bottom of the weaving with enough room to tie off your warps. Weaving from the top down or the bottom up is usually just up to how your brain works and which feels more comfortable to you.

Fig. 1

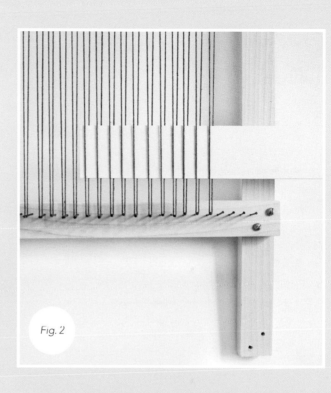

Fig. 2

Tying a Loop Knot

Fold the end of your yarn back on itself 3"
(7.5 cm). Hold the end of your yarn in place with
one hand and tie a knot with the doubled-up
strands so that once it's pulled tight, you create a
loop. You'll also have a tail that you can trim off.

Fig. 3

Oversize Frame Looms

As soon as I felt comfortable with plain weave, the basic over and under of things, I decided I needed to dive into a big project to put my new skills to good use. I pitched a woven-rug tutorial idea to the ladies at *A Beautiful Mess* blog and got the go-ahead without knowing if it would blow everyone's minds or completely fall apart. Sometimes naïveté gets a girl through the right door at the end of the day! I pulled some wood out of my stash and built my first oversize frame loom by ripping sheets into 1" (2.5 cm) strips to use for my warp and weft. It took me two weeks or so in between mom and wife duties, but little by little it came to fruition. That rug is still working hard in my studio space today!

This oversize loom means business! While it may feel a bit overwhelming, consider it a personal challenge to up your weaving game and design something bigger than anything you've ever made before. You can easily adjust the measurements to fit your space or your needs, and you can take it apart once you've finished your project if you use screws to secure it. It's ideal for making rugs of a few different sizes, table runners, statement wall hangings, and larger woven pieces that can be turned into pillow shams or bags. You can use any thickness of yarn you like, but you might also want to consider using strips of fabric, paracord, rope, or other options that will work well depending on your project.

Supplies

2 boards, 2" x 2" x 8' (5 cm x 5 cm x 2.4 m)	9/64 drill bit
2 boards, 1" x 4" x 8' (2.5 cm x 10 cm x 2.4 m)	star-drive bit, optional
12 deck screws, #8 x 2" (5 cm)	handsaw
122 steel finishing nails, 2" (5 cm)	medium-grade sandpaper
power drill	ruler
	pencil
	hammer

Making an Oversize Frame Loom

1   Create your oversize loom in the same way you created your adjustable frame loom. Start by cutting both 1" x 4" x 8' (2.5 cm x 10 cm x 2.4 m) boards in half. You can achieve this with a handsaw at home or politely ask for assistance at a major lumber store, and they'll usually be happy to make the cut(s) for you. Then cut your two 2" x 2" x 8' (5 cm x 5 cm x 2.4 m) boards down to 2" x 2" x 6' (5 cm x 5 cm x 1.8 m). This will create a 4' x 6' (1.2 x 1.8 m) frame, but you can adjust your width and height accordingly.

2 Place your 2" x 2" x 6' (5 cm x 5 cm x 1.8 m) boards parallel to each other about 4' (1.2 m) apart. Then rest one of your 1" x 4" x 4' (2.5 cm x 10 cm x 1.2 m) boards across the top so that the ends are flush. Repeat with a second 1" x 4" x 4' board across the bottom. Place a third 1" x 4" x 4' board in the center (you'll end up with one extra 1" x 4" x 4' board). This will create a rectangle with a center board to help stabilize the frame. This center board also helps make it possible to transport the frame without having it fall over on you!

3 Make 2 marks in each corner where your horizontal and vertical boards meet up. Measure in about 1" (2.5 cm) from the edges and predrill through the top board and into the bottom board (Fig. 1). Repeat for each corner, then drill in your screws (Fig. 2). If you purchase a pack of star-drive deck screws, they should come with a special star-shaped bit.

   Repeat the same process for your center stabilizing board.

   If you don't have access to a power drill, you can replace the screws with sturdy 2" (5 cm) nails, but it will make it difficult to disassemble.

   Sand down any rough places on your frame with your medium-grade sandpaper before starting your next step. This will help keep your fibers from snagging.

Fig. 1

Fig. 2

4 Measure in about 1½" (3.8 cm) from the edge of your top board and make a pencil mark every ¾" (2 cm) until you get about 1½" from the opposite edge (Fig. 3). You should end up with 61 nails in the top board. Repeat the process for the bottom board. Hammer in the nails. If you have any problems with your board showing signs of cracking, you can zigzag your nails all the way across your board so that every odd nail is about 1" (2.5 cm) higher than every even nail.

Warping Your Oversize Frame Loom

5 You'll warp your oversize frame loom exactly as you did your adjustable loom, but you'll need a lot more warp this time (Fig. 4). I suggest using a cone of cotton warp, as you'll be able to warp the entire loom without a yarn break. If you do run short of warp yarn before you're all the way across, just make a loop knot end on the same top or bottom edge as your starting place. Then start another loop knot with your next piece of warp yarn and hook it over the same nail that you ended on. This will help continue the flow of your warp as though it never stopped.

It is much trickier to get an even tension on a larger loom, so be sure to pay close attention to this as you go. You may want to weave in 2 overlapping yardsticks that you'll push toward the top to help even out your tension before starting to weave.

Fig. 3

Fig. 4

Purchasing Frame Looms

Once you're ready to purchase a loom, think about the kind of woven pieces you want to make. Is weaving still just a personal hobby to let you experiment with color and have something to keep your hands busy, or are you hoping to start producing wall art to sell in an online shop? Do you love the process and time commitment of working on larger pieces, or are you interested in compact designs that you can finish after only two episodes of *The Tonight Show*?

There are a variety of loom sizes and designs available online through Etsy as well as many small-business websites. You can choose from laser-cut flat looms made from bamboo in both square and circular shapes, simple lap looms with notches or pegs, standing frame looms that can be placed on a tabletop for a more comfortable weaving experience, and a variety of looms that are designed to be adjustable. Some of them come with kits that include all of the tools necessary, and many shops allow you to purchase tools separately in case you need to replace something.

Learning to weave on a loom you've made yourself is both affordable and satisfying, but there's something to be said for investing in a loom made by someone who has perfected the craft. They'll likely deliver a more finished-looking piece because of precise measurements, and the looms are surely built to last. Do some research, ask some of your favorite weavers what they prefer, and get a feel for your weaving preferences before making your purchase.

This laser-cut portable loom from *The Unusual Pear* is perfect for road-trip weaving.

Chapter Three

Designing Your Woven Project

Any artistic venture requires both motivation and inspiration. Some weavers enjoy the process of sketching out patterns, testing color stories, creating samples, and using templates when they weave. Others prefer to sit down at their loom without a plan, grab whichever fiber is begging to be used next, and allow the design to show itself as it's created. There are as many ways to approach this medium as there are types of people that approach it, and all approaches are valid. Part of the battle is determining which approach you prefer and what steps you need to take to figure it all out. If you prefer to fly by the seat of your pants and find too much planning rains on your creative parade, feel free to skip ahead to your first project and learn as you go. Sometimes you learn best by digging in and figuring it out along the way. Otherwise, feel free to continue reading the rest of this chapter.

Finding Your Style

The first step in figuring out your style is learning what you're most drawn to in the work of others as well as in the natural world around you. The library and the Internet are both excellent tools for discovering and studying traditional designs from certain regions of the world as well as modern designs from established textile artists. Pinterest is a great tool for gathering inspiration, as it is a natural resource for fiber artists and makers sharing their art. If you're able to visit museums with textile displays or see the work of someone in person, you'll be even more inspired by the chance to see how much time and energy went into each piece. Pay attention to why you like something and notice the details in the patterns and designs. What materials are used? Do the colors surprise you? Are there elements in the work that are reminiscent of traditional motifs, or does it feel more abstract and modern?

I regularly troll Etsy and eBay for vintage kilim rugs and daydream about having a house full of them. This fun habit has helped me notice all of the rugs that I love have a few things in common. They all include bold geometric and asymmetrical patterns, usually include pink, indigo, ochre, off-white, and black, and almost never have any orange, purple, or lots of red. Picking up on these similarities has helped me understand what elements I might want to use in my own designs and saves me a little bit of time and energy figuring out the hard way that a wall hanging with purple tones in the design just isn't my thing.

To focus your efforts, create a folder of images on your desktop or on a Pinterest board. Collect images and designs that you're drawn to without overthinking things. Let some time pass and then go back and pay attention to the similarities in all of those images. Do you see a repetition of bold colors or neutrals? Are the tones muted or saturated? Do you lean toward lots of white? Are you noticing certain textures, techniques, or silhouettes you want to test out?

Take design inspiration from patterns and colors throughout your home, around your neighborhood, and in the natural world.

Making Your Style Your Own

One thing to keep in mind as you consume the work of other artists is that we are all learning from the work that has come before us. We have the great responsibility to stand on the shoulders of those giants without forgetting their efforts have allowed us such a beautiful view. As we absorb ideas, patterns, and color pairings, it's important to be mindful in the ways we can contribute something of our own in our work. Makers and artists in every medium will agree that directly replicating the designs and ideas of other artists is a great way to cut our teeth on a new medium, but it is always important to evolve from there and discover what you have to offer. Not only does it respect the hard work and intellectual property of someone else, but it also allows you the opportunity to grow into your own style and share something that will feel deeply satisfying.

One practice I try to incorporate is taking elements of preexisting designs and marrying them to something else. This might be creating a traditional pattern in a modern color story or using a common geometric design in a fresh way. Sometimes it means working with an unexpected material, taking inspiration from the natural world, or stretching the boundaries of a common trend. Deconstruct what you like about something and rethink ways to use those elements. You will inevitably create something more true to yourself that will also inspire others to come up with even different ideas. At the end of the day, each woven piece is a snapshot of the evolution of your design process.

Designing Your Project

Once you are ready to sit down and weave something, there are a few technical things to keep in mind. Do you want to weave a wall hanging or something functional? How large would you like it? Do you have a loom, or will you need to make one to fit that size? Do you know what colors and fibers you would like to use? Do you feel overwhelmed yet? Deep breath.

Try keeping a sketchbook of design ideas and use colored pencils or watercolors to bring them to life. Sometimes the process of thinking design ideas all the way through helps you work out the kinks. It can propel you forward to a better version of your idea. Think about the rule of thirds for the balanced compositions. If you're not already familiar with it, imagine breaking your surface into thirds both vertically and horizontally. The horizontal and vertical lines that define those thirds intersect in four

places. It's scientifically proven that placing focal points along those lines or at those intersections is most pleasing.

Designs are also most interesting and balanced when you have groups of one, three, five, etc. Odd numbers for the win! This can be helpful when you are designing something with a specific number of stripes, layers, or rya knots. Design rules are made to be broken every now and then, but be sure you know the rules so you can break them well.

Using Color and Texture

My favorite part of designing woven projects is choosing colors that sing! Working with the right colors can take a wall hanging from "meh" to "wow." One of the easiest ways to create interesting color stories is to find what is working well in an editorial photo from your favorite magazine. Pay attention to the specific hues and test out ways to replicate them. You may not always find the most interesting fiber tones from big-box hobby stores, so that's just another reason to search out what small-business fiber stores have to offer. Those hand-dyed skeins are hard to beat when it comes to striking colors.

Consider texture for each project you make. Some designs will call for certain thicknesses of yarn. You wouldn't necessarily want to weave your first statement wall hanging from fingering-weight wool unless you aren't interested in finishing it this year. A wall hanging might call for beautiful wool roving, but a rug made from the same stuff might turn into a fuzzy mess.

I Want Candy Wall Hanging

Your first weaving project covers just the basics so you can enjoy the process of finishing a small wall hanging while you get comfortable with the steps involved. Once you've completed this project, you'll know enough about the framework of a woven piece to start to incorporate even more of the techniques taught in the following projects. If you're already pretty familiar with the over and under of things, feel free to work ahead on a more detailed project.

As mentioned in the design chapter (page 30), one of the most important parts in designing your wall hanging is choosing colors you love that also work together beautifully. This simple design has a strong impact in a sorbet palette that feels both modern and fun. A composition with three sections is also easy on the eye as it follows the rule of thirds.

Finished Size

5½" x 13" (14 x 33 cm) including fringe

Supplies

handmade cardboard loom, 6½" x 9½" (16.5 x 24 cm)

worsted-weight hot orange cotton yarn, 5 yards (4.6 m)

worsted-weight rose pink wool yarn, 5 yards (4.6 m)

worsted-weight tangerine cotton yarn, 5 yards (4.6 m)

worsted-weight unbleached cotton yarn for warp, 15 yards (13.7 m)

wooden dowel, 1" x 7" (2.5 x 18 cm)

shed stick

tapestry needle, 7" (18 cm)

tapestry needle, 3" (7.5 cm)

comb

scissors

washi tape

1   Follow the directions on page 20 to create your cardboard loom and then prepare your warp. I'm using white cotton yarn for my warp in this woven piece. Weave in your shed stick from either side of your project by picking up every other warp thread across the warp. You can start by passing over the first warp or under the first warp as long as you continue to go over and under all the way across as shown (Fig. 1). When your shed stick is turned on edge, you will be able to pass the needle or shuttle containing your yarn through the tunnel (or shed) that it creates in one direction. Mine is woven through so weaving from the left to the right is quick work. When I weave from the right to the left, I'll have to pick my way over and under with my needle and fingers.

   Be sure your shed stick is at least 2" (5 cm) wider than your warp width so that it doesn't miss lifting up a warp thread as you work. This could disrupt your over-and-under pattern. When you start using larger looms, you can use a yardstick or thin plank of wood to do the same job.

2   Move your shed stick to the top of your loom for the time being. Thread your needle with about 4' (1.2 m) of tangerine yarn and weave under the first 2 warps on your right side. I prefer not to start weaving from the outer warp thread, also known as the selvedge, as leaving a couple of threads free creates a cleaner edge, and your tail ends don't show when you weave them in on the back side. Weave your needle over the third warp and then under the fourth and continue over and under all the way across (Fig. 2). The tangerine yarn is the first weft yarn.

3   Gently pull your needle and yarn all the way through your warp until you have only a 4" (10 cm) tail left from where you started. As you pull it through, angle it diagonally to create an uphill line (Fig. 3).

4   Carefully pull it down to the base so that there is a slight arc in your weft yarn (Fig. 4).

5   Gently press your weft yarn down in the center and again on either side with your finger to create a squiggly line (Fig. 5).

6   With a comb or with your fingers, push the rest of your weft yarn down so that it's nearly to the base of your cardboard loom (Fig. 6). If it's pretty lumpy, gently pull it more taut and create a new arc. Repeat Steps 5 and 6.

   Using this technique, instead of just pulling straight through to the other side, allows your weft rows to have enough slack in them to maintain an even shape as you work your way up your woven piece. It helps you avoid the dreaded hourglass shape from weft rows getting tighter and tighter until they pull the warp in on the sides. After a few rows of this, you'll get the feel for how much slack you need as you pull it through, and what seems like a lot of fidgeting with each weft row will just become another smooth and possibly therapeutic motion in your weaving process.

7   Going in the opposite direction, weave your needle through (Fig. 7). I end my first weft row by weaving under the last warp so I will be weaving over the top of it and then under the next warp as I continue the over-and-under pattern.

8   Again, pull your weft yarn at an uphill angle as you pull it through. If you want to be sure you aren't pulling too tightly, place a finger on the yarn where it wraps over your outer edge so it stays in place as you create your arc and then your squiggly lines. Repeat the process of pushing your weft row down with your comb or fingers until it is snug against the first row and adjust the weft tension (Fig. 8).

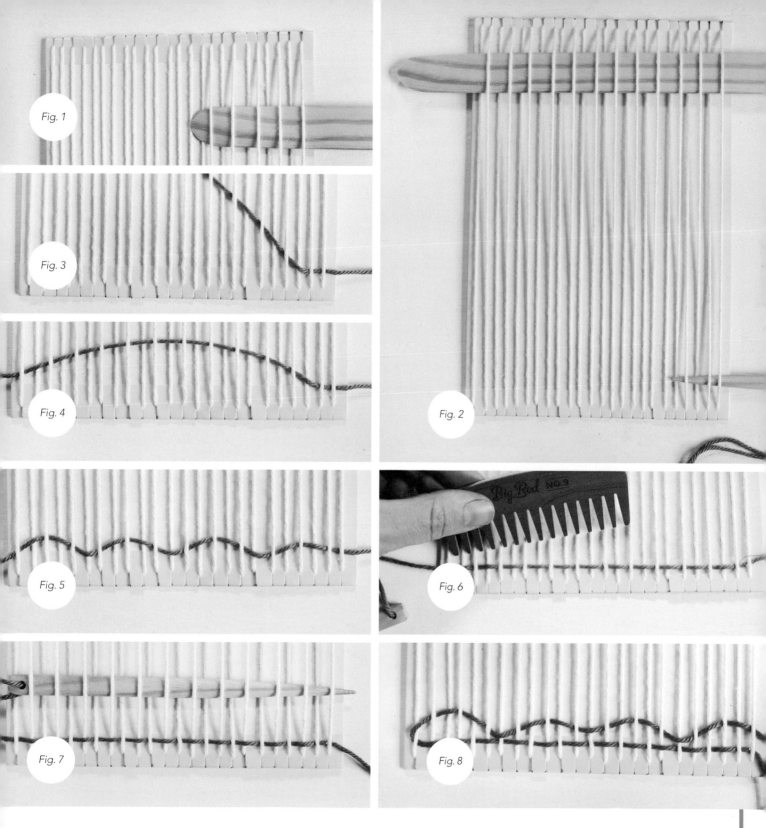

Fig. 1

Fig. 2

Fig. 3

Fig. 4

Fig. 5

Fig. 6

Fig. 7

Fig. 8

9 This is plain weaving in its simplest form! You continue back and forth and back and forth until you run out of yarn. Bring your shed stick down to the center of your loom and tilt it upward as shown (Fig. 9). It will create a shed (or a tunnel) for your needle to pass through without having to finger pick your way through. As mentioned earlier, this works in only one direction on a frame loom. In my case, I can create a shed every time I'm weaving from my left to my right. I simply lift my shed stick and pass my needle all the way through.

10 Once you create a nice little arc, close your shed and move the shed stick back to the top before pushing your weft row down with your comb (Fig. 10). This keeps the shed stick out of the way so you can easily pick your way over and under in the other direction. As you get closer to the top of your project, your warp will get too tight to use a shed stick, and you can just remove it altogether. When you are creating shapes or executing a busy pattern, a shed stick won't prove quite as useful because you'll be changing directions more quickly.

11 Eventually you will run out of weft yarn or decide to change colors. You always want to leave at least 4" (10 cm) of a tail so you can easily stitch it through on the back side (Fig. 11). This keeps your weft from raveling and cleans up all of the ends on the back side of your weaving.

12 Note where the tail end of the first length of yarn is woven under a warp. To add in your next length of weft yarn, thread your needle and pull it up from where the first tail ended and continue the over-and-under pattern. As you can see in the image, the 2 tails cross under the same warp, almost as if there were no break in the yarn (Fig. 12). This helps create a seamless line. This is one of two ways to incorporate the next length or color of yarn. The benefit of this option is that it doesn't create bulk in the weft row, but it can sometimes show a slit behind the warp if the tail ends aren't stitched in well.

The other option is to have them overlap across 3–5 warps and is shown in a few projects later in the book. This can sometimes create bulk in your weft row depending on the thickness of the yarn used, but it avoids having a slit in your design. It's merely a preference based on the thickness of your yarns and the detail of your design.

13 Tuck those tail ends down so they stay out of your way and continue on your merry weaving way (Fig. 13)!

14 Weave 32 weft rows of your first color and then start a thirty-third weft row before changing colors to pink. I suggest switching colors at least a few warps in from your selvedge (the outside warp thread) because it makes for a cleaner edge. This is an example of how it will look when you change colors. Note how the tail ends overlap under the same warp thread (Fig. 14).

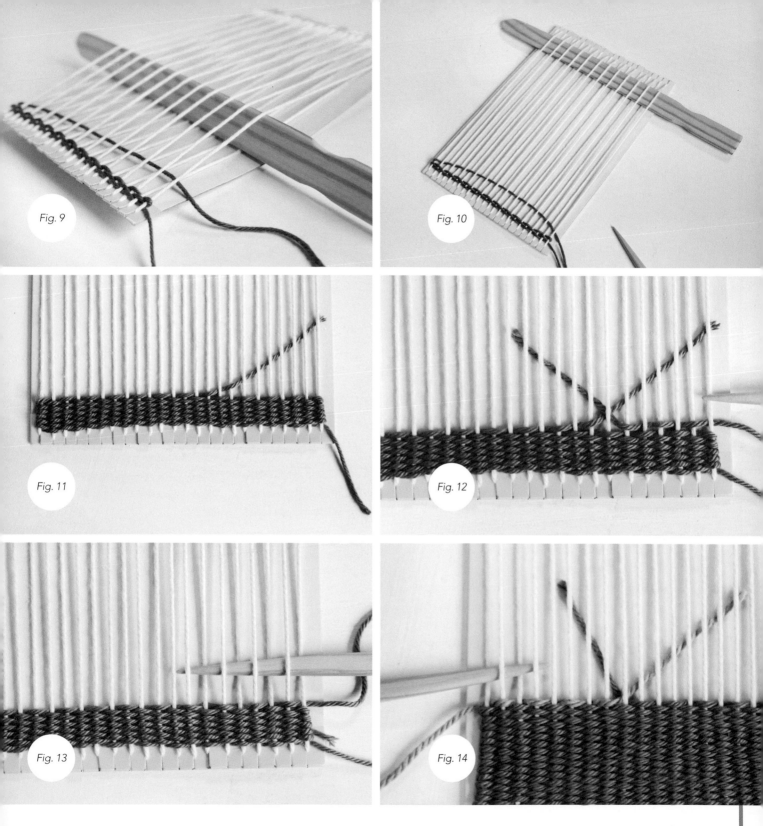

Fig. 9

Fig. 10

Fig. 11

Fig. 12

Fig. 13

Fig. 14

15 This is an example of how a little too much tension on your weft yarn can pull in at the outer warp and eventually distort the shape of your woven piece (Fig. 15). Don't be discouraged if you get halfway through your first project and notice the subtle pulling in at the sides. This happens to almost everyone on their first attempt and is kind of a rite of passage! Consider it a lesson in working out the kinks.

16 Weave in 32½ rows for the pink color block and 32½ rows for the hot orange color block. End your top weft row somewhere in the center and ensure you have a 4" (10 cm) tail (Fig. 16). On a cardboard loom, I suggest leaving about 3" (7.5 cm) of unwoven space near the top, so you have plenty of room to tie your warp threads together as you secure the top of your woven piece. We'll be exploring other ways to finish the rows in future projects, and you'll eventually find a technique that you prefer best.

17 Remove your shed stick if you haven't already. Leave at least 3" (7.5 cm) of space at the top of the tapestry and then cut all the way across the warp (Fig. 17).

18 Tie your warps together in pairs with an overhand knot. If you have an odd number of warps, tie the last 3 together so you don't end up with a lonely warp. Make sure your knots rest on top of the last weft row. If you pull too tightly, you might distort the tension in your weaving and warp the shape of your project, so work with care.

19 Once the top knots are finished, gently pull the threads at the other end off the cardboard loom and tie them in knots as you did at the top to secure the bottom end of your weaving (Fig. 19). You may need to trim the long bottom ends to make sure they are even, but don't cut the top ends.

20 It's time to clean up the back side of your weaving. The best way to finish your tails off is to thread each tail through a small tapestry needle and then stitch it down a warp as shown (Fig. 20). Pull the yarn through, but not so tightly that it bothers the weft row it belongs to, and then trim the excess. Be sure you are stitching through only the back row of your piece and not all the way through to the front. Repeat for each tail.

   The quick-and-dirty alternative to this is to tie your tail ends in gentle knots, but sometimes you'll end up with a lonely tail end. The knots also can keep your weaving from lying flat against your wall or table. Taking time to weave in the ends can feel time-consuming and dull, but it leaves you with a much cleaner back side, and who doesn't love a clean back side? Just saying.

Fig. 15

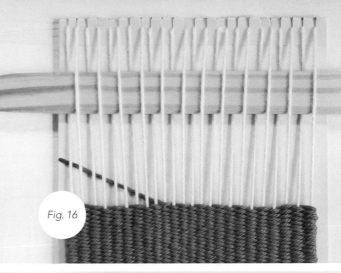

Fig. 16

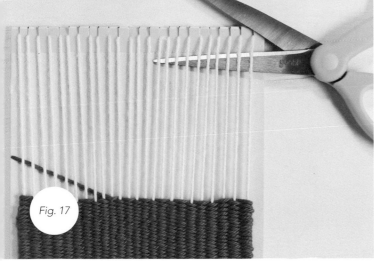

Fig. 17

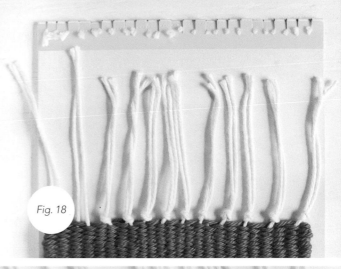

Fig. 18

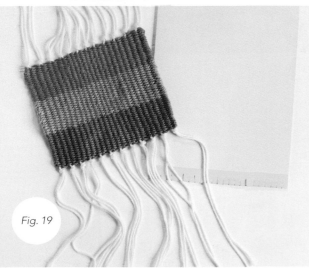

Fig. 19

Fig. 20

21 To create a clean top edge, thread each individually cut warp through your tapestry needle and stitch it down through the weft rows on the back side, as well, after skipping the top weft row (Fig. 21). Skipping the top weft row will keep everything in place on the back side of your weaving. Again, it's a little time-consuming, but skipping this part will leave you with a hot little mess of loose ends that can distract from your beautiful wall hanging.

22 You're finally ready to add your dowel! You can also use a copper pipe, branch, acrylic rod, driftwood, or anything strong enough to support the weight of your weaving. Cut a length of your warp yarn that is about four times the length of your dowel and thread your small tapestry needle. Stitch the yarn under the knot between your first 2 warps on one edge, and tie a knot on the back side. Then wrap the yarn around your dowel and stitch it under the knot of your second set of warps (Fig. 22). Repeat in the same direction all the way across until you get to the last knotted set of warps. Adjust your spacing so that your weaving hangs evenly on your dowel and finish with another knot on the back side. Stitching under the knot between each pair of warps is important because the knots support the weight of the weaving when hung from the dowel.

23 Cut another 12"–14" (30.5–35.5 cm) length of your warp yarn and tie loop knots at each end (Fig. 23). Place them on the ends of your dowel rod, and your weaving is ready to display!

Congratulations on completing your first woven project! Prepare to blow your own mind with how creative you can get once you start incorporating the techniques shared in the next few projects.

Fig. 21

Fig. 22

Fig. 23

Both Ways Wall Hanging

Learning how to create shapes by decreasing and increasing warps is the next step in laying a solid foundation for your weaving designs. Understanding this technique will make your wall hangings much more interesting as you figure out how to use it to execute all of those designs you've been itching to create!

This project shows you how to add shapes by reducing and increasing warps, how to use diagonal slit weave (a second technique for adding in your next row of color), the joys of the hemstitch, and how to add some interest to a simple warp fringe. You can create this kind of wall hanging using a simple cardboard loom, but all supplies listed reference the dimensions of your handmade frame loom.

Finished Size

7½" x 17" (19 x 43 cm) including fringe

Supplies

frame loom, 15" x 24" (38 x 61 cm), set at bottom rung

worsted-weight dark green cotton yarn for warp and weft, 24 yards (22 m)

bulky-weight wool blend yarn in light blue, 4 yards (3.7 m)

single-ply worsted-weight yarn in minty green, 4 yards (3.7 m)

bulky-weight wool yarn in honey, 4 yards (3.7 m)

single-ply worsted-weight wool yarn in highlighter yellow, 5 yards (4.6 m)

worsted-weight off-white cotton yarn, 6 yards (5.5 m)

worsted-weight fleece/wool blend yarn in blue-green, 3 yards (2.75 m)

3 stick shuttles, 8" (20.5 cm)

shed stick, 12" (30.5 cm)

weaving comb

cardboard placeholder, 2" x 12" (5 x 30.5 cm)

wooden dowel, 8" (20.5 cm) long

scissors

Preparing Stick Shuttles

I didn't think I needed to bother with using stick shuttles when I first started weaving. I was happy to cut my yarn to 48" (122 cm) lengths and use a tapestry needle or my fingers to weave; I was pretty pleased with myself for keeping it simple. Finally, I tried wrapping a longer shuttle for a larger wall-hanging design and realized not only do shuttles save time, but they also leave fewer ends on the back to stitch in when I'm finished weaving!

Longer shuttles are great for plain weave when you have big chunks of space to fill in, and shorter shuttles are helpful for smaller parts of your design. I still use tapestry needles when I get into tight places and for finishing off a wall hanging, but I highly recommend purchasing your first set of stick shuttles. Having at least three shuttles will allow you to make progress on a woven piece without having to remove yarn from a shuttle every time you switch colors.

Prepare your shuttles by wrapping them with yarn cut from the skein. If you have more skeins than shuttles, wrap your first shuttles and replace them with a different yarn when you get to that section. You'll begin to get a feel for how much yarn you should wrap once you've used them a few times. Chunkier yarns will create bulk if you wrap too much yarn and will be harder to pass through your shed, so keep the chunkier yarn lengths a little shorter than the rest. If you run out of yarn before finishing a section of your weaving, just add more to your shuttle. You'll still need to weave in your tail ends when you use a shuttle, but you'll have fewer tails to weave.

1 Warp your loom with dark green cotton yarn. Start your loop knot on the sixth nail in from the left and warp across 16 nails total at the top. Weave your cardboard placeholder in and move it up to the halfway point of your warp. We'll be using the bottom of the warp as fringe, so we want to make sure we don't weave it all up. Weave your shed stick in and push it to the top to help even out the tension.

Starting from the right side of your warp, weave in 4 rows of plain weave using the dark green cotton yarn. I always like to end inside the weaving instead of at the edge, so I started a fifth weft row that went down between the second and third warps. This will leave a cleaner edge when you stitch all of the ends in at the end (Fig. 1).

2 Start off where you left off, with light blue yarn, by coming up between the third and fourth warps. Finger pick your shuttle through to the top left corner before gently pulling your yarn down to the bottom left corner to create an arc shape. Then bubble your yarn down with your fingers or a pick and finish your row by pressing it all down evenly with your weaving comb.

To weave in the other direction, slide your shed stick down a few inches (centimeters) and tilt it upward so it holds your shed open. Gently push your shuttle through and up at an angle. Create an arc shape and close your shed. Continue by bubbling and combing your yarn down to create your row. These 2 weft rows will be the only 2 rows of this color that span the whole width of your warp (Fig. 2).

3 Weave your next row to the left, but ignore that last warp before weaving all the way back to the right edge. You've just decreased by 1 warp on the left side (Fig. 3). For this pattern, decrease another warp each time you weave to the left side until you've reached the eighth warp.

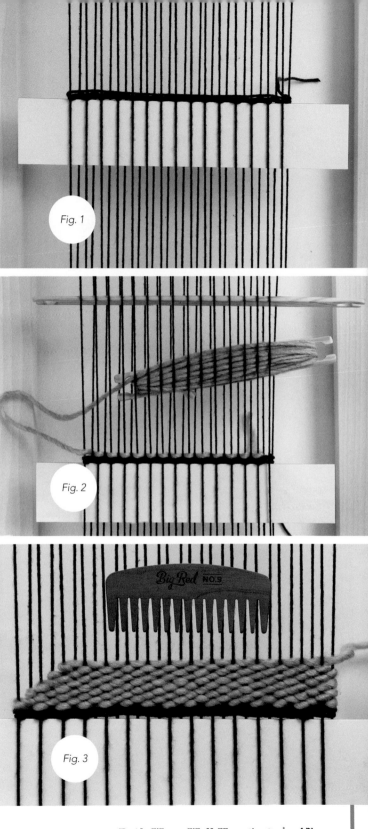

Fig. 1

Fig. 2

Fig. 3

Fig. 4

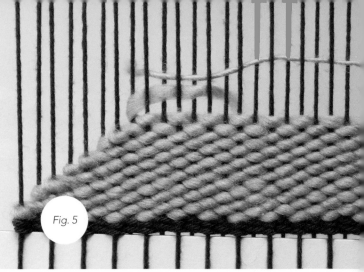

Fig. 5

4 Weave back to the right 5 warps and leave a tail (Fig. 4).

5 A second way to weave in another length of yarn is to overlap it with the previous length. This can be helpful when changing yarn thicknesses, because there is less of a gap where the 2 strands meet behind a warp. Simply weave the new length of minty green yarn in so that it mimics where the previous length has been for about 4 warps and then continue weaving to the edge (Fig. 5).

6 Press the 2 yarns down on top of one another with a weaving comb (Fig. 6). This creates a seamless look between the 2 colors.

7 In the next 2 rows of weaving, increase 1 warp thread to the left. The yarn for this section isn't as thick as the chunky yarn in the last section, so you'll be weaving 2 weft rows at a time before increasing or decreasing a warp (Fig. 7). This will help create even thicknesses of space in your design. It doesn't have to be exact and is only really as important as you want to make it in a geometric design, but it's good to keep in mind how the thickness of your yarn can affect a pattern.

8 In the following 2 weft rows, decrease a warp on the right while also increasing a warp on the left (Fig. 8). Just imagine the same width is shifting over for this section. Keep weaving 2 weft rows at a time until you get back to the outer left warp. This section's shape will be a parallelogram.

9 After you've wrapped your last weft row of minty green around your warp edge, add in your next yarn, in this case the honey yellow yarn, with another overlap (Fig. 9).

10 This yarn is almost as chunky as the first section, so drop back to weaving just 1 weft row per warp increase or decrease. Increase to the right and decrease to the left until you reach the right warp again (Fig. 10). You can see how your negative spaces on the side are looking like triangles, and your colored sections almost look like a folded piece of paper.

11 Weave in another section, this time with the highlighter yellow yarn, and note that your yarn thickness requires 2 weft rows per warp (Fig. 11).

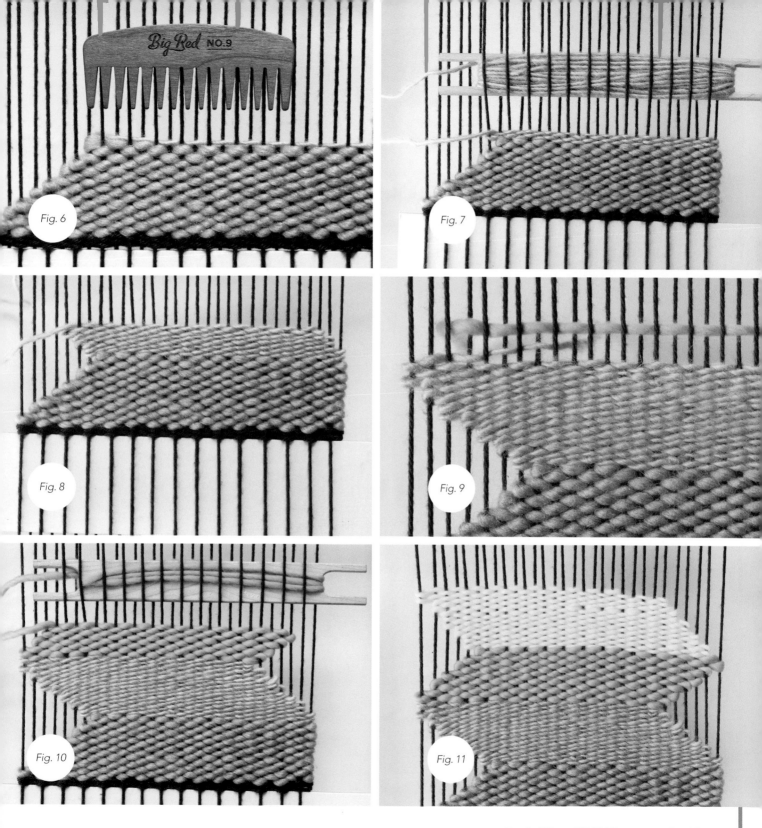

Fig. 6

Fig. 7

Fig. 8

Fig. 9

Fig. 10

Fig. 11

12 Finish the top section with off-white cotton yarn by mimicking the shape of the bottom section (Fig. 12). This means you'll weave all the way to the left edge and increase to the right instead of creating a parallelogram. Weave 2 weft rows per warp.

13 To fill in the negative spaces, thread your needle with about 48" (122 cm) of the dark green cotton yarn and loop it around the outer warp twice (Fig. 13). I usually don't like starting on the edge of a warp, but the design calls for it, so just be sure to give it more attention when you tuck in the tail. There's always exceptions to a rule, right?

When weaving to fill in the negative space, you'll be using a diagonal slit-weave technique. This is where the 2 color blocks rest next to each other on each weft row without locking together. This technique creates a strong contrast between color blocks. It's known as a slit weave because it can leave slits in your piece. When separate color-block edges are woven diagonally in a slit weave, the structure of the weaving is supported by both color blocks, so the slits don't affect much. (We'll use a vertical slit weave in another project, and you can see how it can sometimes be necessary when working with certain shapes.)

Continue to increase 1 warp row for every 2 weft rows as you fill in the negative space.

14 Continue to match the thickness of each row of yarn as best you can. Since the cotton yarn is thinner, it'll require 2 weft rows to match the 1 weft row of chunky yarn. Continue to increase and decrease as you fill in the blanks (Fig. 14) and then end by weaving twice around your outer warp and leaving a 4" (10 cm) tail.

15 Fill in the rest of your negative spaces. Add another 4 rows of dark green yarn at the top to mimic the bottom of the design (Fig. 15).

Hemstitch

16 Finish this wall hanging with a hemstitch. A hemstitch is a clean way of securing your work without having to tie knots at the top. It allows you to rely less on saving enough length at the top when you weave and has a little more elegant look.

This step can be an extension of the same color of cotton yarn, but I changed to the blue-green yarn to make it easier to see where things overlap. You'll need enough yarn to cover about 3 times the width of your wall hanging (Fig. 16). To be secure, your hemstitch needs to have been woven across the width of your wall hanging.

17 With a tapestry needle, weave around the outer warp and behind 2 warps as shown (Fig. 17).

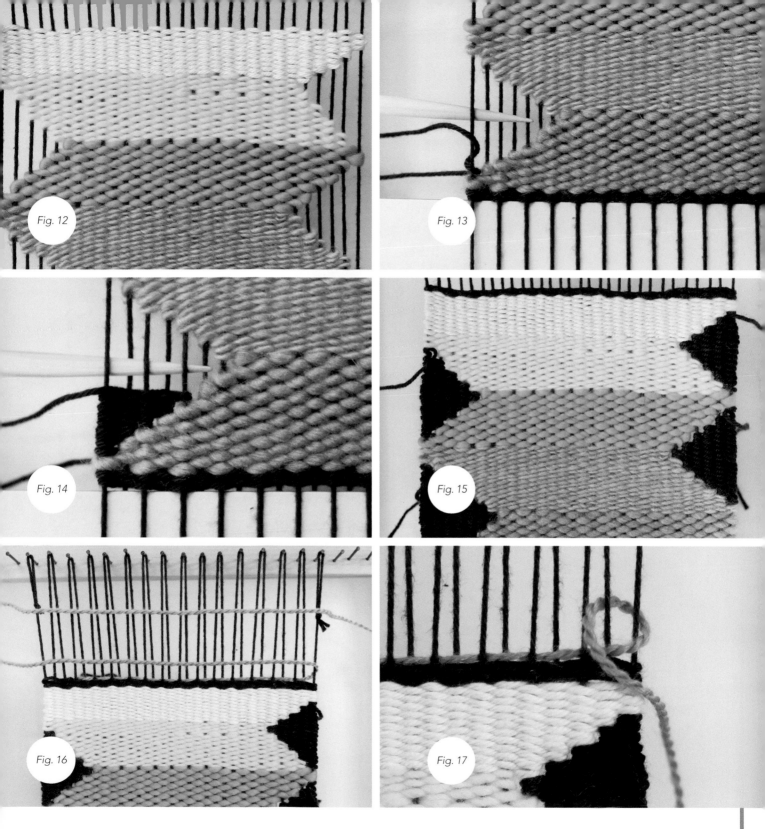

Fig. 12

Fig. 13

Fig. 14

Fig. 15

Fig. 16

Fig. 17

18 Wrap around the front of those 2 warps again and come up with your needle from the back of your wall hanging between the second and third warp and 4 weft rows down (Fig. 18). You can see where I came up between the dark and light rows.

19 Pull the yarn through so that it's snug, but be sure not to distort the width of your wall hanging (Fig. 19). This stitch creates an anchor.

20 Raise your needle up and wrap it behind the next 2 warps (Fig. 20).

21 Then wrap it back around the front of those warps and back again so that you can stitch up from the back of your wall hanging between the fourth and fifth warps and 4 weft rows down (Fig. 21). Pull snugly to create another anchor.

22 Continue all the way across. Check for consistency in the tension of each hemstitch knot as you work (Fig. 22).

23 Once you get to the other side, wrap around the outer 2 warps and then again to the back, but stitch between the first loop and the warps to create a knot (Fig. 23).

24 Repeat that motion for another knot. Leave a 4" (10 cm) tail so you can stitch it in when you clean up the back side (Fig. 24).

25 Carefully remove your cardboard placeholder and unhook your warp from the loom (Fig. 25).

26 Cut your warps at the bottom where they loop and then tie them in a knot close to the base of your weaving (Fig. 26). You can leave this as is or add in a little macramé to create an interesting pattern. It

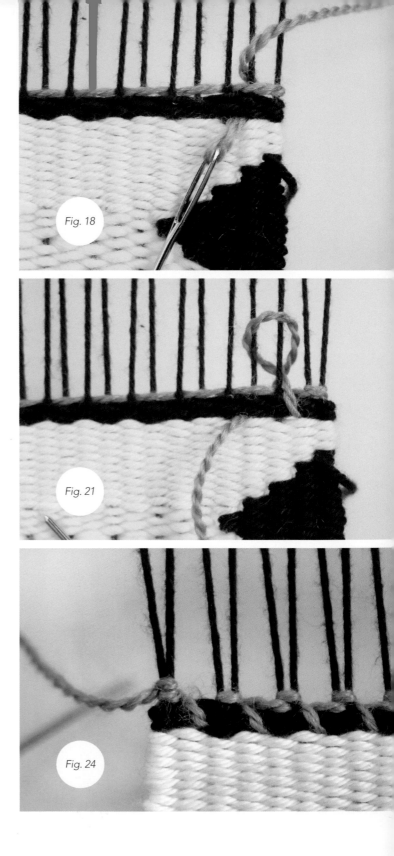

Fig. 18

Fig. 21

Fig. 24

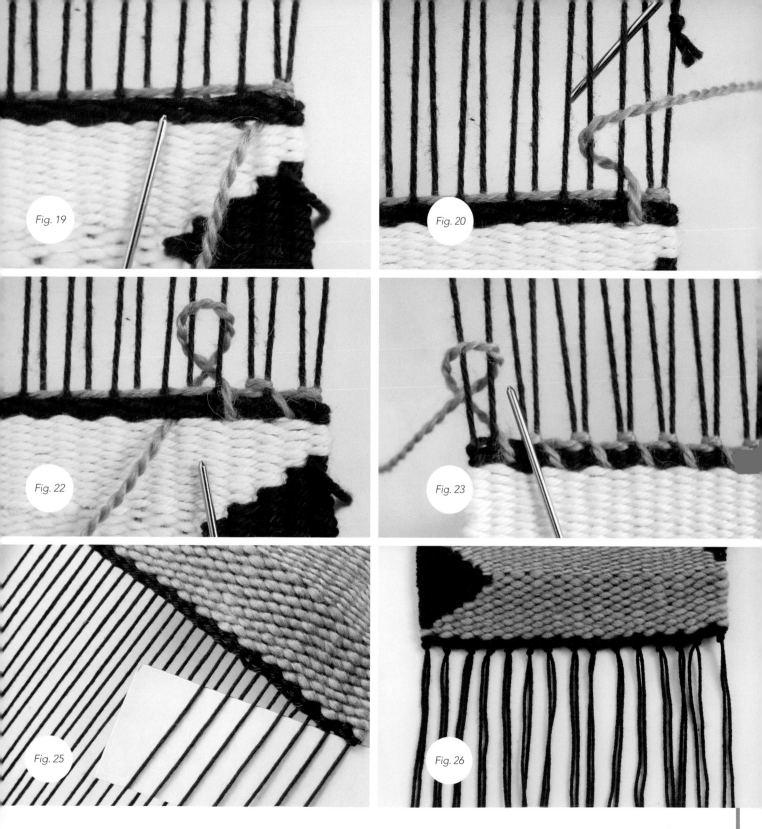

Fig. 19

Fig. 20

Fig. 22

Fig. 23

Fig. 25

Fig. 26

will shorten the length of your fringe just a little, so keep that in mind if you're already happy with the length.

Macramé Design

27 To add the macramé, separate the 2 strands per knot. Combine the 2 closest strands between the first knotted section and the second knotted section and tie another knot about ½" (1.3 cm) down (Fig. 27).

28 Repeat all the way across. Double-check that each knot is consistently about ½" (1.3 cm) down from the previous row of knots (Fig. 28).

29 The very first and last strands won't be included in the knotting for this row (Fig. 29). You can continue with another row of knots in the same fashion or leave it as is. Adding macramé is just another easy way to customize your wall hangings to make them more interesting.

   Whether you added macramé or not, trim your ends so they are even and clean up the back of your weaving by stitching in your tails and the top warps, as you were shown on pages 40–42 in the first project. Stitch your wall hanging on to a hanger of your choice and display it proudly!

Now that you know how to create shapes by increasing or decreasing warps, you'll be able to plan out more complicated designs or even just create more movement when you design as you weave.

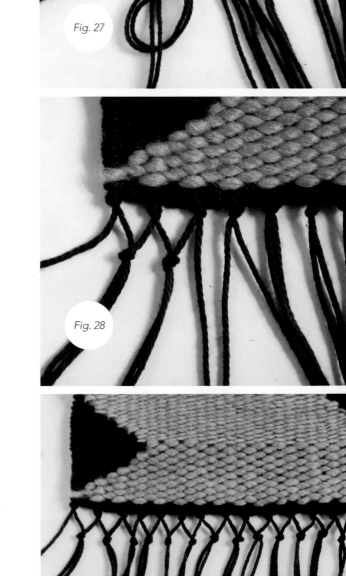

Fig. 27

Fig. 28

Fig. 29

Opal
Wall Hanging

In this wall hanging project, you'll learn to create layers of fringe and learn how to weave a triangle shape in order to create angled fringe. Each fringe is made up of rya knots, a Scandinavian word describing the traditional rugs made using the type of knot that creates a double-sided pile of yarn. These can be cut to your desired length and made with a variety of thicknesses for different effects. They add a lot of color to each wall hanging and create depth and interest when layered on top of each other or over sections of plain weave.

Finished Size

10" x 18" (25.5 x 45.5 cm) including fringe

Supplies

wooden frame loom, 15" x 18" (38 x 45.5 cm)

worsted-weight cotton yarn in cream for warp, 20 yards (18.3 m)

sportweight wool yarn in dark gold, 90 yards (82.3 m)

worsted-weight wool yarn in red, 90 yards (82.3 m)

worsted-weight, two-ply, wool/cotton blend yarn in pink, 70 yards (64 m)

worsted-weight cotton yarn in green-blue, 30 yards (27.4 m)

worsted-weight wool yarn in cream, 18 yards (16.5 m)

copper pipe, 12" (30.5 cm) long

shed stick

tapestry needle, 6" (15 cm)

tapestry needle, 2½" (6.5 cm)

wooden comb or fork

cardboard placeholder, 2½" x 12" (6.5 x 30.5 cm)

scissors

1. Warp your loom with cream cotton yarn for a total of 38 warps and weave in your cardboard placeholder. Weave about 8 rows of green-blue cotton yarn (Fig. 1). These rows act as a support for the first row of rya knots and help bind all of your warps together once the project is taken off the loom.

Rya Knots

2. Cut the strands of dark gold yarn for the bottom row of rya knots to about 24" (61 cm) long each (Fig. 2). You'll need 7 strands of yarn per rya knot, which will be 14 strands when folded in half. There are 38 warps on this wall hanging. Each rya knot will fold around 2 warps, so you'll divide 38 by 2 to get 19. You'll need 19 rya knots with 7 strands each for a total of 133 strands of yarn measuring 24" long.

   If doing math takes all of the fun out of this for you, feel free to just cut the same length of yarn 7 times per rya knot until you fill all of your warps. You'll likely need to trim these for an even edge, so don't fret too much over specific measurements. If you are using a chunky yarn, you'll likely want to use fewer strands, as they'll each take up more room. Likewise, if you're using a fingering or lace weight, you'll want to use more strands to maintain a full rya knot.

3. Center your 7 strands on top of 2 warps (Fig. 3). I like to start from the outer edge and work my way to the other side if I'm working all the way across. If you're not adding rya knots all the way to the edge but want them centered on your piece, find your center 2 warps and work out from there.

4. Reach between your 2 warps and pull all 7 strands from the right side up through the middle without pulling so tightly that it doesn't stay centered. Fold them to the same side they came from (Fig. 4).

5. Reach through the same 2 warps and grab the 7 strands on the left side. Pull them back up through the 2 warps and fold them back to the left side (Fig. 5).

6. Gently pull on the loose ends to tighten your loop into a neat knot. If one or more of your strands is looser than the rest, gently tug on one strand at a time to find which one is loose and then pull it until it rests evenly with the rest of the group. You might have to work a little bit at getting your knots to look neat at first, but this will soon become one quick movement. Wham, bam, done. Once your knot is neat, move it down until it rests snugly on top of your last weft row (Fig. 6).

7. Continue this process all the way across your loom until you have a full weft row of rya knots (Fig. 7). You may want to trim these at the bottom for a clean edge, but I suggest waiting until your woven wall hanging is finished, so you can see how it will hang before taking scissors to it.

8. Create some height in your design before adding in the second row of rya knots by adding in 54 rows of plain weave with green-blue yarn (Fig. 8). This can be in any color you have on hand, but a coordinating color is always best in case it happens to peek through your rya knots. Use a shed stick and either a tapestry needle or shuttle to make quick work of this section. Be sure to press each row down with a comb or fork as you work.

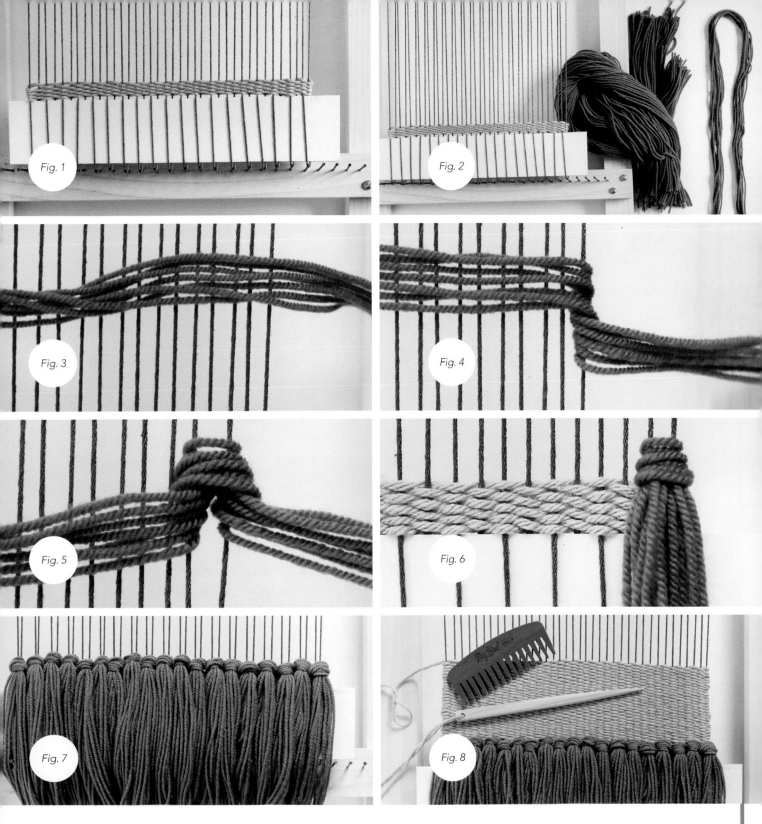

Fig. 1

Fig. 2

Fig. 3

Fig. 4

Fig. 5

Fig. 6

Fig. 7

Fig. 8

9 Cut the red yarn lengths for your next layer of knots so that it covers the plain weave as well as about half of the bottom row of knots. For this project, cut each strand to about 21" (53.5 cm) long and use 7 strands per rya knot for a full effect. You can create a straight line across or cut your knots into an angled design, but you'll want to make sure you're working with enough length to give yourself some options. Continue adding your rya knots all the way across your warp, pressing them down gently as you work (Fig. 9).

10 This next section's purpose is to create more height in the design for the next layer of rya knots, but this time the knots will angle up like an arrow. To create this shape, create about 2" (5 cm) of plain weave all the way across your warp with green-blue yarn. Reduce your next 3 weft rows by 2 warps on both the right and left sides. This means your next 3 weft rows will leave out the outer 2 warps on both ends (Fig. 10).

11 Continue to reduce by 2 more warps on both sides for every 3 weft rows you weave. This will create a stair-step pattern on both sides that meets in the center of your warp. In the middle, weave between your center 2 warps 3 times. Tuck your end between the warps and make any minor adjustments to be sure the left and right sides are even.

This is one of the methods you will use in a later project to create shapes in your plain-weave designs. You can reduce by 1 weft row or 10 weft rows. You can mirror the same pattern or just work your way in one direction. You can add in the same amount of warps for every 3 weft rows to create an upside-down triangle as you work up your piece.

Cut your next bunch of rya knot strands so that they are long enough to completely cover the foundational plain weave and overlap onto the second

layer of knots by at least 2" (5 cm) from the highest point of your triangle. For this project, cut the pink strands about 12" (30.5 cm) long and use 8 strands per knot. This will create enough bulk from a slightly leaner 2-ply strand. Tie rya knots onto the stair steps; they'll create a fun arrow shape (Fig. 11). You can also cut them to meet in an even row at the bottom, but you'll need to measure them out 1 knot at a time.

12 Continue adding all of your rya knots up your stair-step triangle. Your ends will need trimming for a cleaner look. Start trimming from the outer rya knots on each side and work your way up (Fig. 12). Trim off the same amount on all of your knots for consistency. Raise 1 rya knot up at a time from the rest of the fibers to make sure you don't accidentally trim off the layer behind it.

13 Fill in the rest of the warp space with plain weave in whatever color suits your preference. I went with a worsted-weight wool in cream to help the bolder colors tell the story. Start weaving in between the outer 2 warps on the right side near the bottom of your stair-step space and weave in 3 weft rows before adding in the next 2 warps.

Continue adding in 3 weft rows up and 2 warps over until you can weave straight across over the top of the highest rya knot. Keep weaving back down the other side of your stair step to fill in the negative space (Fig. 13).

14 Once you've filled it in down to the last 2 warps on the left side, tuck the yarn end between the 2 rows so the end rests on the back side (Fig. 14). Adjust your weft rows that may get pushed up to make room for your needle to work through.

Fig. 9

Fig. 10

Fig. 11

Fig. 12

Fig. 13

Fig. 14

Fig. 15

Fig. 17

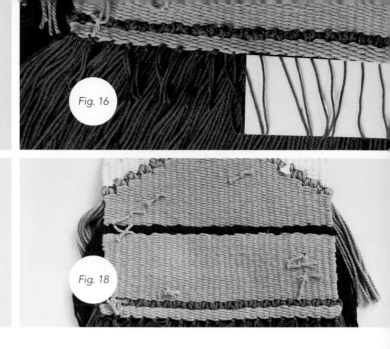

Fig. 16

Fig. 18

15 Cut another strand of the same yarn and add in another 1"–2" (2.5–5 cm) of plain weave at the top. It should look pretty seamless so that you can't see that you worked in sections.

You should still have at least 3" (7.5 cm) of space between your top weft row and your nail heads. Add a hemstitch (page 50) to finish off the top of your weaving for a cleaner line. To get it off the loom, cut your warps as close to the nail heads as possible and then tie the warps together two at a time in a knot (Fig. 15).

If you have less than 3" (7.5 cm) of space, you may just want to pull the warps off of the nail heads and wrap them around your dowel or copper pipe 1 loop at a time.

16 Remove the cardboard placeholder at the bottom of your loom after you've pulled those loops carefully off the nails, and tie your warps together 2 at a time in a knot (Fig. 16). They should be knotted snugly against your bottom row of plain weave to secure the weaving.

17 Stitch your dowel or copper pipe onto the top of your wall hanging and add a yarn hanger.

Hang your woven piece up to see how your fringe lies. Use your fingers or your weaving comb to brush out and straighten the strands and then trim as you see fit (Fig. 17). I like to hang my woven piece against a door that has some woodwork that allows me to follow a straight line from one side to the other. You can also rest your wall hanging flat on a square or rectangular table with the bottom layer hanging over the edge. You can use the edge as a guide to cut a straight line.

18 This is what the back of your piece will look like (Fig. 18). Stitch down your loose warp ends at the top of your weaving through the top few rows of weft with your 3" (7.5 cm) tapestry needle as shown on page 42. You can also stitch in the loose ends of cotton and wool yarn that you used for your plain weave for a finished look, but you can also sometimes get away with tying these together in knots and trimming your ends if they aren't so bulky that they cause a bump in your wall hanging when it's flat on the wall. Consider it a shortcut if you're short on time or motivation!

This is a great project if you want to make a large wall hanging without spending a lot of time on a woven design.

Group Hug Wall Hanging

Weaving with roving not only makes quick work of things, but it's also a unique experience. Wool roving is wool that has been cut and carded in preparation to be spun into yarn. It comes in long sections that are usually 2"–3" (5–7.5 cm) thick and can be used for felting as well as weaving. It's so soft you'll literally want to curl up and fall asleep in it. This woven piece uses an undyed bundle of roving, but you can find it in a variety of your favorite colors or experiment with dyeing it yourself.

Wool roving will add a great deal of texture and depth to your wall hangings. Use it in small sections to help break up the composition of your piece or fill your entire warp. It can be used in place of spun yarn for a fringe or can add plenty of drama when stitched directly on top of plain weave.

Finished Size

16" x 25" (40.5 x 63.5 cm) including fringe

Supplies

frame loom, 15" x 18" (38 x 45.5 cm)

worsted-weight unbleached cotton yarn for warp, 20 yards (18.3 m)

undyed merino wool roving, 8–10 ounces (226.8–283.5 g)

single-ply worsted-weight yarn in minty green, 25 yards (23 m)

light worsted-weight yarn in amber, 150 yards (137.2 m)

bulky-weight wool yarn in cream, 70 yards (64 m)

copper pipe, 14½" (37 cm) long

cardboard placeholder

shed stick

tapestry needle, 6" (15 cm)

tapestry needle, 3" (7.5 cm)

scissors

1. Warp your loom with the unbleached cotton yarn for a total of 50 warps, then weave in your cardboard placeholder. Add 6–8 rows of plain weave using your unbleached cotton yarn to help secure the bottom section of your wall hanging (Fig. 1). Remember to leave a 4" (10 cm) tail of yarn on the back side wherever you finish so that you can stitch it in when you add the finishing touches to your wall hanging.

2. Cut your light worsted-weight amber yarn into 24" (61 cm) strands. You'll need 8 strands per rya knot and a total of 25 rya knots. Make each rya knot (page 58) and gently push it down so it's resting snugly on top of your plain weave (Fig. 2). You'll likely want to trim the ends of these for an even edge once your wall hanging is complete for a cleaner look.

3. Tie your next layer of rya knots from the bulky cream wool yarn all the way across (Fig. 3). Each of your 25 rya knots will need 4 strands measuring 20" (51 cm) long. You'll need fewer strands here because this yarn is bulkier than the first layer of knots. You can add plain weave in between your layers of rya knots to create height, but I skipped that step and layered them directly above the first row of rya knots. Again, you'll likely want to trim the ends of your knots after you've taken your wall hanging off of your loom.

4. Tuck one end of your roving in between the first and second warps on the right side to give the roving section a clean edge. I usually tuck in my roving ends 2 warps in from the edge, but since I had 2 rows of rya knots, there would've been a little bit wider of a gap, and I didn't want it to wedge down in between the 2 rows of rya knots.

   Bring your roving around and under the single outer warp (Fig. 4). You'll weave 2 warps at a time for the rest of this wall hanging, so pass over the next 3 to help even things up. This will be the only spot you'll weave 3 at a time in this project. Weaving through 2 at a time using roving allows for a little more room for it to bubble and loop without being so tightly squeezed that it pushes your warps out too far.

5. As you work, be sure you gently pass your wool roving under your warp threads. Pulling too hard could create snags in your roving for a fuzzy section. I like to use one hand to pull the loose end through and my other hand to help raise up the shed space between the warps. I don't tend to use a shed stick for this part, because I like to take my time shaping the bubbles and loops that the roving can make in between warps. Experiment with twisting your roving and pulling up different-sized sections as you work across your loom (Fig. 5).

6. As you work back to the right side of the loom, be sure you're weaving through the opposite 2 warps at a time from your first weft row (Fig. 6). This helps secure the structure of your wall hanging despite it having a little extra wiggle room from a looser weave. You can experiment with weaving under 4 warps for a little variety every now and then, but if you have too many, you will lose some of the integrity of your structure.

Scrap Yarn Tip

You can use a loosely tied scrap of yarn to help you mark color changes or keep track of counting your rows if you're designing a specific shape. You can see the yarn I used to mark the center warps in Figure 3. Simply cut off the scrap when its job is done.

Fig. 1

Fig. 2

Fig. 3

Fig. 4

Fig. 5

Fig. 6

7   Once you get to the end of your roving, tuck in a 3" (7.5 cm) tail behind your warp (Fig. 7).

8   Add in your next section by overlapping under the same warp as usual but with a slightly longer tail. This time, bring your tail up and mimic the same pattern of over and under that your last section of roving made before tucking in a 1" (2.5 cm) tail behind your warp (Fig. 8). When you press this down, it will blend with your last section of roving so that there isn't an odd bubbling gap. Once your tail is sorted out, you can continue weaving over and under the opposite of the weft row underneath.

9   Weave 2 rows of roving all the way to the selvedge before reducing to create a bit of an hourglass shape. Decrease by skipping the outer 2 warps on both the right and left sides for the third weft row and then skipping the outer 4 warps on both the right and left sides for the fourth weft row (Fig. 9). Repeat this for the outer 6 warps and outer 8 warps. This will be the narrowest point of your hourglass shape. Your next weft row should add in 2 more warps at a time on both the left and right sides. Continue in this fashion until you have wrapped around the outer warps on both sides.

10 Press each weft row of weaving down as gently and tightly as you can to help secure the structure of your wall hanging (Fig. 10). Weaving a worsted-weight yarn through the negative space on the sides will add in some support as well as color.

11 Once your roving section is complete, thread your small tapestry needle with the minty green single-ply worsted-weight yarn and fill in the blanks. Start with your yarn tail in between the first 2 warps and weave 10 or more quick weft rows until you are able to weave across the next 2 open warps. Then weave back and forth about 10 more weft rows or until you can weave across to include the next 2 warps (Fig. 11). Continue filling in the negative space by weaving another 2 warps until you need to start reducing as you move higher up your woven piece.

12 You can count your weft rows in this section as you increase or reduce warps, or you can just eyeball how many rows to add as you fill in your negative space. Leave a 4" (10 cm) tail to stitch through the back side after you finish the rest of your weaving (Fig. 12).

Fig. 7

Fig. 8

Fig. 9

Fig. 10

Fig. 11

Fig. 12

13 Repeat the same process on the opposite side of your warp and fill in the negative space (Fig. 13). You can weave from the top down or the bottom up. Once you've finished, step back and even out your shapes with your fingertips so that both sides match.

14 Thread your tapestry needle with any leftover wool or cotton yarn and weave 3 rows right above the wool roving (Fig. 14). Make sure you press the rows down firmly but without upsetting the shape of your wall hanging. This will help lock things in place while you remove your wall hanging from your loom.

15 If you have about ½" (1.3 cm) of space between your last weft row and your nails, you can carefully pull each warp loop off the nail and onto your copper pipe (Fig. 15). The warp loops will fit snugly, and this will continue to keep the rows locked in place. If you don't have enough room, simply remove the warp loops and hemstitch them (page 50) onto the copper pipe or other material you might use in its place.

Remove your cardboard placeholder and tie your bottom warps in overhand knots so they rest snugly under your weft rows. Continue cleaning up your wall hanging by stitching in the loose ends and gently tucking in any fluffy strands of roving. This is also a great time to give your wall hanging a haircut and trim your layers of fringe.

Create a hanger from your cotton yarn and enjoy!

Fig. 13

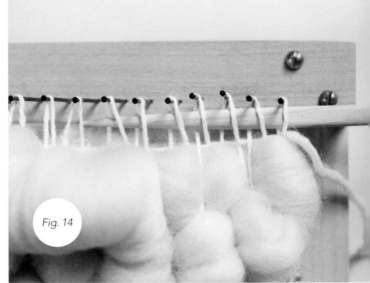

Fig. 14

Fig. 15

Band Wife Wall Hanging

Rya knots aren't just for neat little rows! This project shows you how to fill your warp with them to create a touchable sculpture that will add incredible texture to your wall space.

When designing a rya weaving, consider the ways you want your yarn to lie. Plan out longer layers on the bottom and shorter layers on the top to conserve yarn, or just trim the strands after you've finished the entire piece. Create movement by working in abstract sections or weave in straight rows for a completely different look. This project is all about playing with texture, colors, and the overall silhouette of your wall hanging.

Finished Size

12" x 23" (30.5 x 58.5 cm) including fringe

Supplies

frame loom, 12" x 16" (30.5 x 40.5 cm)

worsted-weight single-ply cotton yarn in natural for warp and weft, 11 yards (10 m)

bulky-weight single-ply wool yarn in natural, 30 yards (27.4 m)

bulky-weight single-ply wool yarn in dark blue, 10 yards (9.1 m)

light worsted-weight two-ply wool yarn in gray-blue, 20 yards (18.3 m)

heavy worsted-weight chained linen yarn in powder blue, 10 yards (9.1 m)

worsted-weight two-ply yarn in aqua, 15 yards (13.7 m)

worsted-weight single-ply cotton yarn in aqua, 7 yards (6.4 m)

worsted-weight single-ply yarn in minty green, 5 yards (4.6 m)

worsted-weight single-ply wool yarn in natural, 5 yards (4.6 m)

copper pipe, ½" x 9" (1.3 x 23 cm)

cardboard placeholder, 2" x 12" (5 x 30.5 cm)

shed stick, 12" (30.5 cm)

stick shuttle, 8" (20.5 cm)

tapestry needle, 3" (7.5 cm)

scissors

1. Warp your loom with 23 warps in the natural worsted-weight cotton yarn, insert your cardboard placeholder, and weave 8–10 rows of plain weave for structural support (Fig. 1). This won't show once it's hung, so the color isn't too important.

2. Cut your bulky natural yarn into 6–8 strands per rya knot that measure 18"–24" (45.5–61 cm) long to create a substantially dense base section For a more interesting sculptural effect, you'll want to incorporate some longer layers at the very base and then cut shorter lengths as you work your way up. Center each set of strands over the top of 2 warps and wrap each side around and pull them back through to the top side of your weaving. You don't need to add these evenly across your warp, but it does help to work in sections.

   Your first section of bulky yarn in natural will cover the bottom right corner of your warp and include 8 rya knots as the first weft row, 6 rya knots as the second weft row, 5 rya knots as the third weft row, and then 2 rya knots as the fourth weft row (Fig. 2).

3. You could very well add layers of rya knots on top of each other all the way up your warp, but then there would be nothing to secure the warps to each other and the piece would not be structurally sound. To ensure this doesn't happen, you can overlap warps with your rya knots and even skip a warp every now and then. Just be sure you don't leave a lone warp on the outer edge, because it may not be aesthetically pleasing. Another option is to work in horizontal sections and then weave in 2 or 4 rows of plain weave every 3" (7.5 cm) or so. This will ensure the structure of your wall hanging is secure.

   Cut 3 or 4 strands per rya knot measuring about 14" (35.5 cm) long in dark blue yarn and add in two rya knots on the first weft row right next to the natural rya knots. Then add in another dark blue rya knot with 3 or 4 strands that measure about 28" (71 cm) long and

place it directly above one of the dark blue rya knots in the first weft row. Add a second rya knot next to it using the same dark blue, but keep those strands shorter at about 20" (51 cm) long. Place it directly above the other dark blue rya knot in the first weft row (Fig. 3). You can trim these strands individually later to make them a little more varied. Finish filling in the space left over on the first 2 weft rows with more rya knots of the bulky wool yarn in natural. Continue filling in your weft rows using varied colors and textures.

4. A quicker way to add in rya knots is to cut 1 long length of yarn and then fold it in half 2 or 3 times. This saves time because you don't have to cut individual strands and then trim them later. Here I used gray-blue light worsted-weight yarn (Fig. 4).

5. Add your rya knot and then cut your loops so that the bottom layers of the loop are slightly longer than the top layers for a layered effect (Fig. 5).

6. Cutting the loops this way will add in some bulky layers (Fig. 6).

7. Vary lengths and thicknesses of your rya knots as you work your way up the warp (Fig. 7). You can vary the number of strands per yarn depending on the thickness you'd like in a specific section of your wall hanging. If you have a thinner, lighter weight yarn, you may want to use twice as many strands as you would for a bulky yarn for a substantial effect. If you'd like a more delicate effect, use fewer strands. Also, varying the weights of yarns adds much more interest and texture to your wall hanging.

8. Add some depth to your wall hanging by filling in spaces with plain weave using powder blue worsted-weight linen yarn (Fig. 8). This not only reinforces the structure of your weaving, but it also adds even more texture and interest.

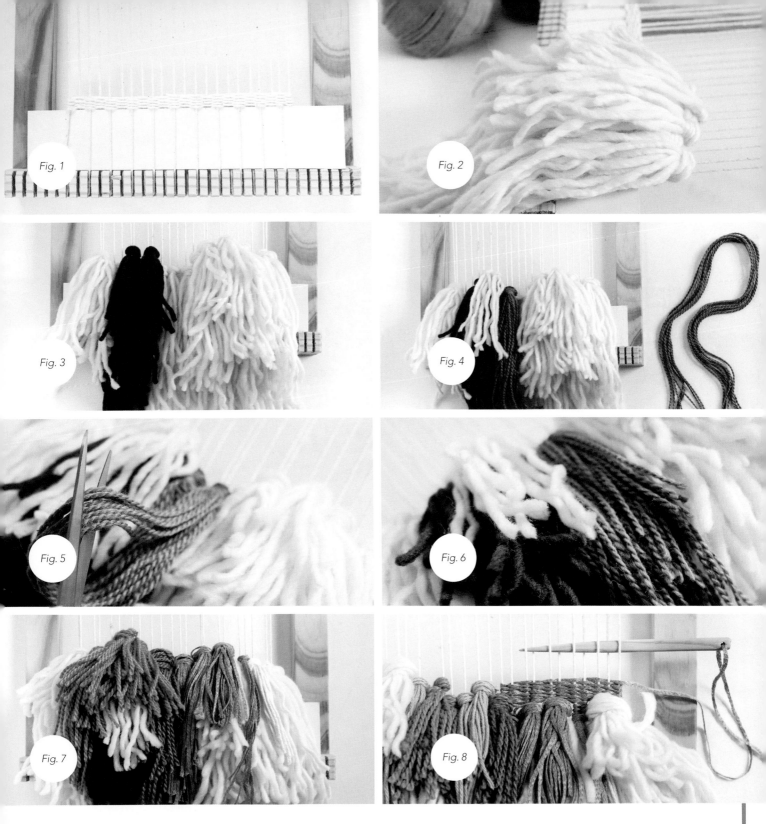

Fig. 1

Fig. 2

Fig. 3

Fig. 4

Fig. 5

Fig. 6

Fig. 7

Fig. 8

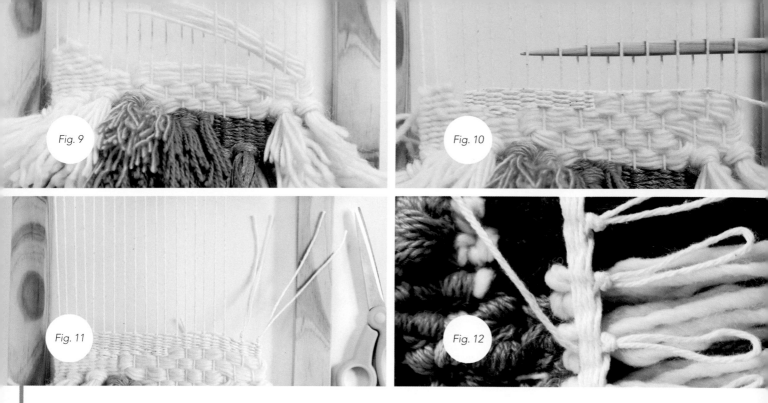

Fig. 9

Fig. 10

Fig. 11

Fig. 12

9   Weave an abstract section of wool yarn on the left side and then fill it in on the right side with a grouping of natural wool yarn strands (Fig. 9). This means you'll be weaving with more than one strand of yarn at a time. These won't all fit through a tapestry needle at once, so I suggest using a stick shuttle for this section.

10 Finish off the top of your piece using natural cotton yarn. Fill in any gaps and then continue across the full width of the warp for a handful of rows to help secure the structure of the wall hanging (Fig. 10).

11 Cut your warp threads and stitch them through the back side. Secure the top of your weaving with a hemstitch or tie each pair of warp threads in a knot close to the last weft row (Fig. 11).

12 Remove the cardboard placeholder and knot the warps at the bottom snugly against the first row of weaving (Fig. 12).

13 Stitch your wall hanging around the hanger of your choice and add to your favorite corner. Once you've got it hanging, you can see where you might want to trim up some of your rya knots.

I love how much this looks like an explosion of yarn. It's a quick weave if you want something that will have a big impact without spending all weekend on it. It's also a great way to use leftover yarn strands from your stash or previous weaving projects.

The Stars at Night Wall Hanging

Are you feeling brave enough to tackle something a little more complex? This project uses the skills you've already learned, such as plain weave, creating shapes, rya knots, layering, and hemstitch, and takes all of those up a notch. On top of that, you're about to learn how to add even more dimension to your wall hanging with the looping technique as well as the soumak stitch. Adding in either of these two new elements will infuse so much more interest into your designs, and they are dynamic enough to be used in a variety of weaving styles. In case that wasn't enough new information for you, you'll also learn to interlock your weft rows when designing shapes. Watch out, world! We're about to get fancy!

Finished Size

13" x 23" (33 x 58.5 cm) including fringe

Supplies

frame loom, 18" x 24" (45.5 x 61 cm)

worsted-weight single-ply cotton yarn in cream for warp, 34 yards (31 m)

worsted-weight single-ply wool blend yarn in minty green, 43 yards (39.3 m)

worsted-weight single-ply cotton yarn in cream for weft 90 yards (82.3 m)

sportweight two-ply wool blend in amber for weft and fringe, 30 yards (27.4 m)

fingering-weight two-ply wool in dark green, 70 yards (64 m)

laceweight single-ply wool in powder blue, 58 yards (53 m)

worsted-weight two-ply cotton yarn in cream, 63 yards (57.6 m)

bulky-weight single-ply wool yarn in cream, 50 yards (45.7 m)

bulky-weight single-ply wool yarn in honey, 2 yards (1.8 m)

worsted-weight two-ply cotton yarn in coral, 10 yards (9.1 m)

sportweight two-ply wool yarn in cranberry, 4 yards (3.7 m)

alpaca roving in natural white, ¼ ounce (7 g)

dowel or pen, ¼" (6 mm) diameter

copper pipe, 14" (35.5 cm) long

cardboard placeholder, 2" x 26" (5 x 66 cm)

stick shuttle, 12" (30.5 cm)

stick shuttle, 8" (20.5 cm)

weaving comb

wooden weaving needle

tapestry needle, 8" (20.5 cm)

tapestry needle, 3" (7.5 cm)

scissors

1 Warp your loom with 50 warps using cream cotton yarn as you have in previous projects so that you start and end your loop knots on the top of your frame. Weave your cardboard placeholder through and gently push it to the bottom of your frame. Add about 6 rows of plain weave with the same yarn (Fig. 1).

2 Create a unique silhouette with a fringe full of rya knots that is narrower than the width of your warp. Cut 5 strands of minty green wool yarn each measuring roughly 24" (61 cm) long for each rya knot (page 58). Start from the center 2 warps and work your way out to each side for a total of 13 rya knots.

Fill in the negative space on the right side of your warp with more plain weave until you reach the same height as your rya knots. Weave all the way across your warp to the outer left warp. Carefully weave down to fill in the negative space using a needle because your shuttle won't fit into the tight spaces. Gently press your rows down until they are even with the rya knots (Fig. 2).

If you prefer, you can also just cut your yarn after you've woven all the way across so that it has a tail. Start a new length of yarn to weave up toward that tail and then just press the top row and tail down with a comb.

3 Weave about 2" (5 cm) more of plain weave to create height before adding your next layer of rya knots (Fig. 3).

4 Using the dark green yarn, add in 7 rya knots on both sides of your warp (Fig. 4). Each rya knot should contain about 10 strands of yarn measuring roughly 13" (33 cm) long. This yarn is a fingering weight, so it's rather thin and is a nice contrast to the thicker wool strands below.

5 Fill in the center space with more rya knots of a different yarn weight and color. For this project, use the amber yarn to make 11 rya knots with each knot containing about 6 strands each measuring roughly 20" (51 cm) long (Fig. 5). You want to make sure these rya knots are longer than the ones next to them but shorter than the ones below them. You'll likely trim these at a later stage, so don't fret too much over this part.

6 Use your stick shuttle to weave 2" (5 cm) more of plain weave using the cream cotton yarn to add in height before tying your next row of rya knots.

For each of these 3 rya knots, cut 30 strands of the laceweight powder blue yarn with each strand measuring about 28" (71 cm). Center these 3 knots on the warp (Fig. 6). When using thicker rya knots for visual interest, skip a warp in between each rya knot to make sure each knot at the top has a little wiggle room and isn't pushing warps out of the way. These knots need to be shorter than the very first row of rya knots but longer than the row directly underneath. All of this overlapping keeps your eye moving and makes your weaving look pretty incredible already!

7 Fill in the sides with more rya knots using 2-ply cream worsted-weight cotton yarn (Fig. 7). I chose a lighter color to give my eye a rest as it moved up the wall hanging. From the yarn, cut 7 strands measuring about 12" (30.5 cm) long for each knot. This layer will get trimmed up at an angle at a later step while the rest of them will be trimmed straight across.

Looping

8 Before adding loops into the design, create 4 rows of plain weave with the bulky cream yarn for structure between the rya knots and the loops.

You'll need something round such as a dowel, knitting needle, or pen for this step. Weave a loose weft row with the bulky cream yarn and gently pull your yarn up between the first 2 warps and wrap it over your dowel. Then gently pull that same strand up from between the next 2 warps and wrap it around your dowel in the same direction as you wrapped the first loop. Continue gently pulling up and wrapping your yarn over your dowel in between each warp until you get to the rya knot. Adjust the yarn so it is wrapped evenly for consistent loops (Fig. 8). Don't remove your dowel just yet!

9 Be sure your yarn wraps around a warp before returning it in the other direction to weave 1 row of plain weave (Fig. 9).

10 Firmly press your plain-weave row down so that it rests snugly against your looped row (Fig. 10).

11 Gently pull your dowel out from your loops (Fig. 11). Press your plain-weave row down again with your comb to make sure your loops are locked in place. Add in 2 more rows of plain weave to create more structure and give your loops a little breathing room, or just leave 1 row of plain weave in between each row of loops. If you don't add in at least 1 plain-weave row, your loops will get wild on you and slip out of place when moved. No one likes disobedient loops.

12 Continue adding loops while reducing your next loop row by 2 warps; mimic its width with your plain-weave row (Fig. 12).

> ## Looping Tip
> You can create loops using more than one strand of yarn for an even thicker patch, and you can adjust how high they loop depending on the thickness of your dowel or similar tool.

Fig. 7

Fig. 8

Fig. 9

Fig. 10

Fig. 11

Fig. 12

Fig. 13

Fig. 14

13 Create orderly little rows of loops that decrease by 2 warps on both sides to make room for something fun in the center of your wall hanging (Fig. 13).

Soumak Stitch

The soumak stitch can be used to fill in large portions of your wall hanging or just add variety in small portions. Be aware that it will require more yarn per inch (centimeter) than usual, as you're traveling back and forth as you work your way in one direction. I like to refer to it as the reverse Bruce Springsteen stitch because you take two steps forward and one step back instead of the way The Boss wrote it. In this variation, I am actually taking four steps forward and two steps back.

14 Start with about 36" (91.5 cm) of bulky-weight honey yarn and thread it through a tapestry needle. Tuck the tail end up between the second and third warps (Fig. 14). We'll fix him later.

15 Tuck your tail down toward the looped section. Working from left to right, wrap your needle over the top of the warp so that you pass over 4 warps and then tuck it back to pass under 2 warps (Fig. 15).

16 Gently pull your yarn through. You don't want to cause your warps to bend at all during this back-and-forth process, so keep things a little loose (Fig. 16). You'll be able to adjust as you get familiar with how it's turning out.

17 Starting from where your yarn came out, wrap it to the right over another 4 warps and then stitch back under 2 warps to the left (Fig. 17). Gently pull your yarn through.

18 Repeat (Fig. 18).

19 Keep stitching 4 forward and 2 back until you reach your preferred warp thread (Fig. 19). If it's not quite 4 forward and it's only 3 forward, no worries. Instead of going back 2 warps, just wrap around the last warp once to help you switch directions. If you weave another row of soumak in the opposite direction, you'll end up with a braided or herringbone-looking pattern. Or you can just add a row of plain weave.

20 Since I ran out of warps on my last soumak row, I mimicked my pattern and stitched over 2 and then stitched back 2 to even it up (Fig. 20).

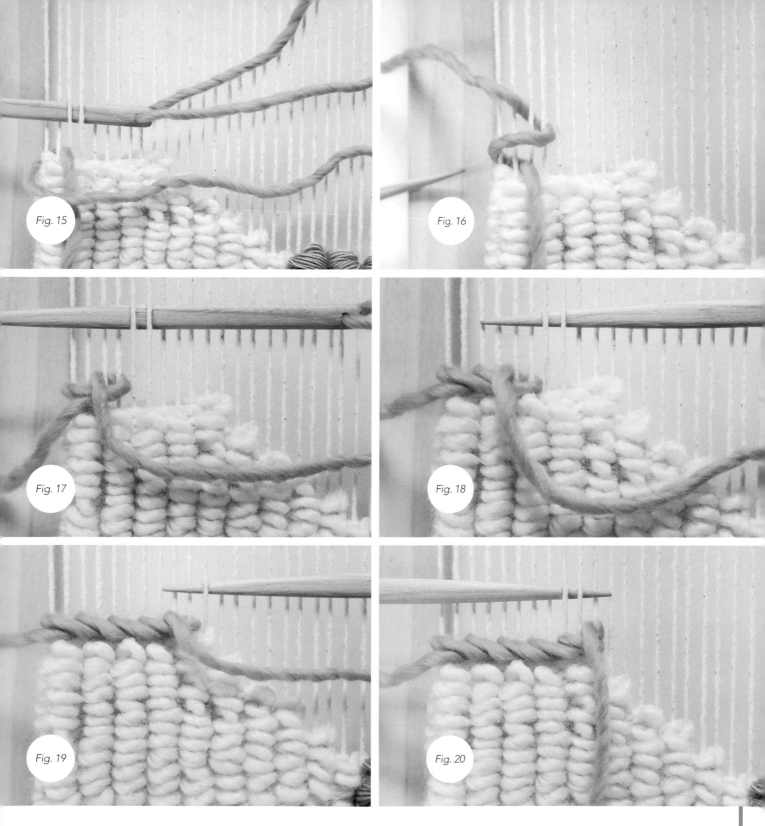

Fig. 15

Fig. 16

Fig. 17

Fig. 18

Fig. 19

Fig. 20

Fig. 21

Fig. 22

21 Resume the pattern of 4 forward and 2 back (Fig. 21).

22 You can see the pattern pretty clearly here (Fig. 22).

23 I wanted a little more thickness in my color block, so I decided to go for 2 more rows of soumak. I treated the outer 2 warps as a single and wrapped around them twice before moving forward. To mimic the same pattern as the first soumak row, wrap over the next 2 warps and then back behind the same ones to get back on track (Fig. 23).

Soumak can feel a little confusing when you're switching directions, but you'll get comfortable with it soon enough.

24 Here is the full color block of 6 total rows of soumak stitching (Fig. 24). Wrap those tails around and tuck them in to the back using the finishing stitch technique (Step 20 on page 40).

25 Repeat on the opposite side of your warp (Fig. 25).

26 Fill in the bottom of your negative space with coral cotton yarn using the slit-weave technique (page 50). This time it's more vertical than diagonal. You can see the space it creates between the cotton yarn and the looped wool yarn. It still gets just enough support by moving at a diagonal angle every few warps, though. Fill about 12 rows of coral yarn and set aside.

Create a star motif with the cranberry yarn by creating a row of plain weave that covers 12 warps in the middle of the coral yarn and then decreases by 1 warp on each side until it covers only 2 warps. This is the bottom triangle of the motif. Weave out 10 warps to the right before returning to the left for 22 warps. This is the second layer of your motif that you'll reduce by 1 warp on either side for 7 weft rows (Fig. 26).

27 Create a mirror image as you finish the rest of your motif. Keep your rows spaced as evenly as you can despite the fact that your shape is floating in negative space right now (Fig. 27).

Interlocking Color Blocks

28 As you continue your coral cotton yarn in the direction of your cranberry yarn, instead of just letting it wrap around the warp next to your cranberry row, stitch through the cranberry row where it loops back (Fig. 28). This doesn't count if you have a tail end, such as the one shown on the start of my cranberry color-block shape, as there is no loop to interlock through, only a tail end. In that case, continue with the slit weave as usual.

Fig. 23

Fig. 24

Fig. 25

Fig. 26

Fig. 27

Fig. 28

29 Plain weave back to the right and then come back to the left again. Every time you meet a loop from the cranberry color block, stitch through it and then wrap around the warp either over or under like you would regularly (Fig. 29).

30 As you can see, the 2 color-block weft rows interlock in between the warps (Fig. 30). This changes the line of the design a little so that it's not such a strong contrast. But it does provide for a tighter weave and plenty of structural support. This is an excellent choice when you're weaving with thinner yarns, such as the ones used, as there won't be a lot of extra bulk at the interlock. It takes longer to make that extra little stitch, as you have to use a needle instead of a stick shuttle, but it's another technique to tuck away for future genius design ideas.

31 Fill in the rest of your star motif and then experiment with more looping, more plain weave, and a variety of yarn thicknesses for some more textural interest near the top. Add in 3 or 4 rows of plain weave before finishing your wall hanging with the hemstitch (page 50) (Fig. 31).

32 Take your project off the loom. Stitch in the loose ends on the back, attach the dowel of your choice, and trim your rya knots as you prefer them.

Enjoy your fancy new wall art!

Fig. 29

Fig. 30

Fig. 31

Poesy Wall Hanging

This darling wall hanging is so soft and textural, it makes me want to run my fingers through the fringe! In this project, you'll learn to use negative space in your weaving as part of the design as well as another few ways to use the soumak stitch. The design isn't quite as complex as the last project, but the tonal colors and use of negative space make it plenty interesting.

The key to working with negative space is to provide enough structure around your negative space for your warps to stay in place. You can do this by wrapping warps with a weft yarn to define a boundary, working with thinner fibers to create a dense block of weft around your negative space, and keeping enough weight in the spaces below your negative space to keep your warp taut. There's so much to learn by experimenting with negative spaces in your design.

Finished Size

13" x 25" (33 x 63.5 cm) including fringe

Supplies

frame loom, 18" x 24" (45.5 x 61 cm)

worsted-weight two-ply cotton yarn in natural for warp and weft, 15 yards (13.7 m)

bulky-weight single-ply wool yarn in coral, 70 yards (64 m)

worsted-weight two-ply cotton yarn in cream, 57 yards (52.1 m)

bulky-weight single-ply wool yarn in light pink, 59 yards (54 m)

bulky-weight single-ply wool yarn in light gray, 18 yards (16.5 m)

bulky-weight single-ply wool yarn in honey, 7 yards (6.4 m)

worsted-weight two-ply wool yarn in variegated orange, 7 yards (6.4 m)

laceweight single-ply wool yarn in powder blue, 30 yards (27.4 m)

wooden dowel, 1" x 12" (2.5 x 30.5 cm)

cardboard placeholder, 2" x 16" (5 x 40.5 cm)

stick shuttle, 12" (30.5 cm)

stick shuttles, 8" (20.5 cm)

weaving comb

7" (18 cm) wooden weaving needle

3" (7.5 cm) tapestry needle

scissors

1 Warp your loom with 46 warps of worsted-weight cotton yarn in natural. Weave in your cardboard placeholder, add 6 rows of plain weave for structural support with the warp yarn, and get to cutting your first row of rya knots from the bulky coral yarn. Each rya knot should be made up of 6 strands of bulky wool yarn measuring about 16" (40.5 cm) long. You will use fewer strands because of their bulk. Had they been worsted weight or thinner, you would've included 8 or 10 per rya knot. Make 23 rya knots total (Fig. 1).

2 Add in about 3" (7.5 cm) of plain weave using the cream cotton yarn to add height before your next row of rya knots (Fig. 2).

3 Cut the bulky wool yarn in light pink to create 23 more rya knots; for each knot, cut 6 strands measuring about 12" (30.5 cm) long each. Make the knots across the warp (Fig. 3).

4 Mark your center 2 warps with scrap yarn and add in 3 more rya knots that are centered on your warp. Use the bulky wool yarn in light gray and cut 6 strands measuring 32" (81.5 cm) for each knot. Tie the 3 knots (Fig. 4). Note that these knots will be longer than your bottom row of rya knots by a few inches (centimeters).

5 Add in 12 (or more) weft rows of cream plain weave until you can increase your warps by 2 just above the rya knot. Add in 12 more weft rows of plain weave before reducing again by 2 warps (Fig. 5). Continue reducing by 2 warps every 12 weft rows until you have 5 stair steps.

6 Repeat on the opposite side for a mirror image (Fig. 6). This section is looking quite similar to the last project but isn't quite as complex.

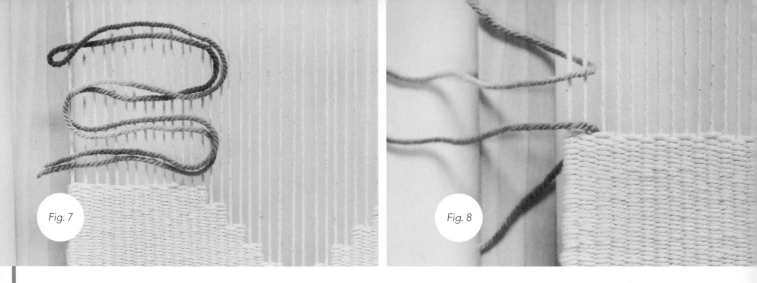

Fig. 7

Fig. 8

Soumak-Stitch Variation

7   Cut the worsted-weight yarn in variegated orange so that it is about 4 times the width of the row you want to weave when folded in half, or about 12" (30.5 cm) for this design (Fig. 7). We're going to do a variation of the soumak stitch here that almost feels like cheating. It's a way to weave 2 rows at once! I'm a fan of anything that saves a little time, so this soumak variation has become a new favorite technique.

8   Start with both tail ends tucked down between the third and fourth warps so that your yarn is resting to the left (Fig. 8).

9   Wrap your yarn under and bring it up between the third and fourth warps (Fig. 9).

10   Weave it back 2 warps (Fig. 10).

11   Weave it down between the first and second warps and gently adjust your yarn loops so that they are consistent with each other (Fig. 11). Your top and bottom rows will need to stay separate for now so you can continue to weave in between them, but you'll be able to press them down at the end.

12   Weave under 3 warps to the right and up and back 2 warps to the left (Fig. 12).

13   Continue until you run out of yarn (and start again with a new length where you left off) or until you reach the preferred warp (Fig. 13).

14   Wrap the yarn around your preferred warp thread (decreased by 2 to follow the design from the plain weave) and tuck the loop tail so that it's on the back side. Gently push the top row of soumak down onto the bottom row for a herringbone pattern (Fig. 14). Repeat on the opposite side.

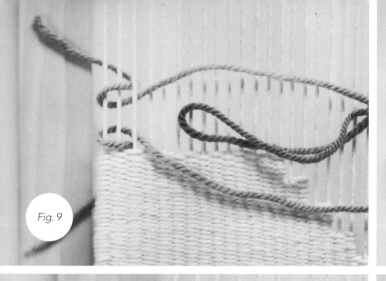

Fig. 9

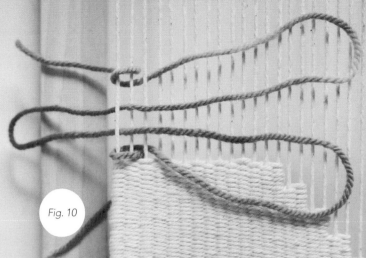

Fig. 10

Fig. 11

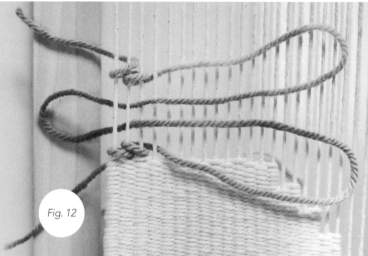

Fig. 12

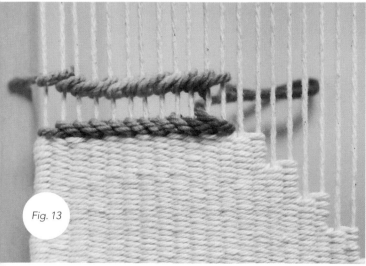

Fig. 13

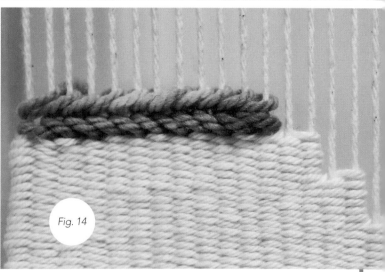

Fig. 14

15 With the cream cotton yarn, add in 2 more stair steps of plain weave above the soumak-stitch rows, by continuing to reduce 2 warps every 12 weft rows.

Add rya knots on each stair step using the bulky wool yarn in honey (Fig. 15). Since this is a bulky yarn, like that used for the rest of the rya knots, use 6 strands for each knot. Cut each strand to about 10" (25.5 cm) long. You'll trim these up later. Cut enough strands for 15 rya knots.

16 Fill in the space between the honey-colored rya knots with slit weave using the bulky wool yarn in light pink until just before you reach the top of the fourth row of rya knots (Fig. 16). The light pink yarn is chunky, so you'll have fewer rows than if you were using a thinner yarn. Continue to press each weft row down with your weaving comb to keep things snug and consistent. This is especially important when building color blocks around a negative space.

17 Your last full row of weaving for this space should cover the top of your fourth rya knot on the right side. To create a stair-step pattern and your negative space, weave back to the left but only by 6 warps. This means you'll stop before you get to the 2 warps in the center of your weaving that your bottom rya knot is wrapped around. Keep this color block of space even with the height your rya knots create. With a bulky yarn, that means you'll shift to the next stair step on the right on every sixth weft row and decrease on the left of that same weft row. This maintains an even stair step. Once you reach the space above the top right rya knot, weave out to the right edge for 4 more rows (Fig. 17).

18 Mimic the same pattern on the opposite side. Adjust your 2 sides with your fingers and your weaving comb so that they are evenly spaced before moving on to the next step (Fig. 18).

19 Cut a 36" (91.5 cm) length of the variegated orange yarn and wrap it around the center right warp as many times as you need to match the height of the yarn next to it. Since this yarn is a thinner yarn than the bulky yarn in the stair-step pattern, you will wrap around your warp 4 times (Fig. 19).

To weave across the top of a stair-step pattern, weave a backward soumak stitch where you'll wrap around the back of the weaving to go 2 to the right and 1 to the left. The soumak pattern will show up on the back side, but mostly it's acting as a place-holder on the front side to keep the boundaries of your last color block in place and to create a pattern from your negative space.

20 Continue up to the top of that last stair step and weave out to the right side. Wrap your tail end in a few warps. Repeat the same process on the oppo-site side of your negative space. Use the same color yarn to weave up another 1" (2.5 cm) of plain weave to create a color block on top of the negative space to help define the area even more (Fig. 20). This provides the structure needed just above the nega-tive space for things not to pull out of place and lose their shape. Add another row of soumak at the top of this plain weave using 3 warps forward and 2 warps back. This elongates the stitch for a stronger contrast against the plain weave.

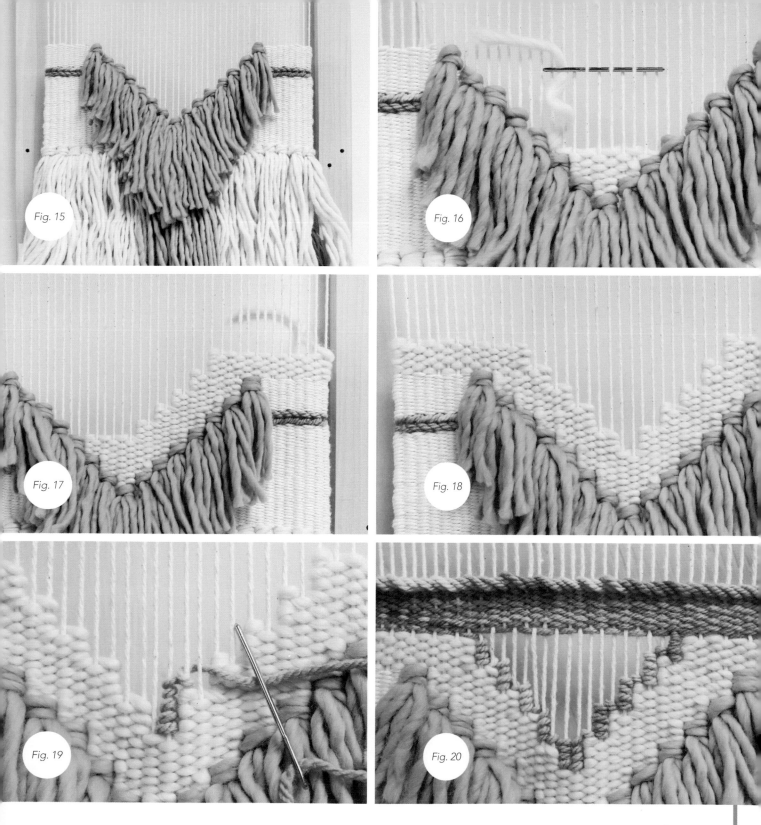

Fig. 15

Fig. 16

Fig. 17

Fig. 18

Fig. 19

Fig. 20

21 Bundle about 30 strands of powder blue lace-weight yarn that measure about 2½ times wider than your warp and weave it in a soumak stitch with 4 warps forward and 2 warps back. Gently tie knots around the outer 2 warps and leave a 3" (7.5 cm) tail for interest. Instead of pressing this down against the coral soumak-stitch row, leave a little space (Fig. 21). You'll see why in the next step.

22 Leave about ½" (1.3 cm) of space above the powder blue soumak row and add in 1" (2.5 cm) of cream plain weave. This will keep your warps evenly spaced at the top of your wall hanging and provide more structure for the negative space you'll be creating. Gently move your powder blue soumak row up your warp so that it's snugly pressed against your plain weave. This will create about 1" of negative space below (Fig. 22). The bulk of your soumak stitch above, combined with the plain weave, will offer plenty of structure, and the weight of the wall hanging below the negative space will keep your warp threads taut.

23 Hemstitch (page 50) just above your plain weave to lock it all in and remove your weaving from your loom. Add your dowel, stitch in the loose ends, and trim your fringe to your preference (Fig. 23).

You've now created a project with plenty of depth and texture and have seen a few other ways to include a soumak stitch to create interesting lines and patterns in your design. Don't forget to experiment with the silhouette of your wall hanging. What other ways might you let your fibers run loose off of your warp?

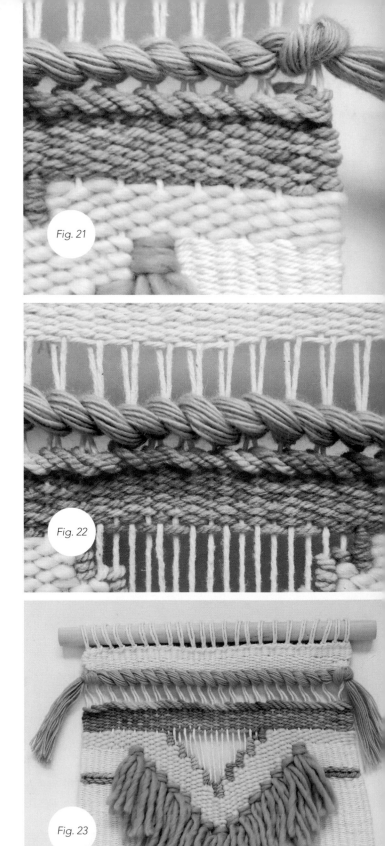

Fig. 21

Fig. 22

Fig. 23

Triple Scoop Wall Hanging

This fun, pop art design was inspired by ice cream, Venn diagrams, and my love for tonal colors. It reminds me of trips to our local drugstore to get Thrifty ice cream in a cone. I always got sherbet back then. I love this piece's mod vibe and how different it is to the wall hangings with layers of fringe, looping, and rows of soumak. It relies less on texture and dimension and more on the colors and shapes in the design.

In this project, you'll learn to design with a cartoon, or template, to create a tapestry-like wall hanging, and I'll also take the mystery out of weaving circular shapes on a grid. With these tools, you'll be able to design outside the boundaries of straight lines and stair steps for even more unique woven wall art.

Finished Size

11" x 30" (28 x 76 cm) including fringe

Supplies

frame loom, 15" x 18" (38 x 45.5 cm)

worsted-weight two-ply cream cotton yarn for warp and weft, 60 yards (55 m)

light worsted-weight two-ply wool/alpaca blend in amber, 95 yards (87 m)

sportweight two-ply wool/silk blend in honey, 30 yards (27.4 m)

light worsted-weight two-ply wool yarn in mint blue, 12 yards (11 m)

light worsted-weight two-ply wool yarn in mint green, 19 yards (17.4 m)

worsted-weight two-ply poly blend yarn in light peach, 12 yards (11 m)

light worsted-weight two-ply cotton yarn in coral, 30 yards (27.4 m)

sheet of paper, 13" x 18" (33 x 45.5 cm), for a template

dinner plate, 8" (20.5 cm)

fine-point black permanent marker

acrylic dowel, 1" x 12" (2.5 x 30.5 cm)

cardboard placeholder, 2" x 16" (5 x 40.5 cm)

stick shuttle, 12" (30.5 cm)

stick shuttles, 8" (20.5 cm)

weaving comb

7" (18 cm) wooden weaving needle

3" (7.5 cm) tapestry needle

scissors

1. Create a template, also called a cartoon, for your design to help guide your pattern as you weave. The purpose of this cartoon is to keep your design on track so you don't get halfway through and realize you started shifting too much to the left or that the circle in the center is much too tall and now looks like an egg. To create this design, place an 8" (20.5 cm) dinner plate in the center of your paper and trace around it with a marker or pen. Then trace another dinner plate–sized circle above and below it so that the edges overlap the first circle without touching each other in the middle. If you prefer, trace with a pencil first and then outline with a marker. Be sure your outer edges are even so that your woven design is even.

   Warp your loom with 46 warps using the worsted-weight cotton yarn in cream and place a shed stick or cardboard placeholder at the bottom to hold space to tie off your warp ends (Fig. 1).

2. Place your cartoon behind your loom and then choose your colors (Fig. 2). Due to the nature of a Venn diagram, this design is best showcased when the overlapping colors are similar to one of the two colors in the individual circle they share. You don't have to have the perfect color blends in the overlapping circles but maybe just a slight variation in the tone. I suggest you use yarns in similar thicknesses for this pattern for color-block shapes that match each other. Thinner yarns, such as a fingering or light worsted weight, will create a more defined circular shape than chunky yarns.

3. You can leave your cartoon behind your weaving for reference, but I prefer to trace my cartoon pattern onto my warp to help guide my curved lines (Fig. 3). It takes out some of the guesswork when you're trying to line things up as you go. The marks on your warp should get covered with your weft yarn, so they won't likely show, but keep the possibility of the marks showing in mind when you choose a color to mark with. Place a few books under your cartoon so that it's pressed up against the warp and carefully trace your pattern. You'll still want to reference your paper cartoon every now and then to make sure things are still staying in place, so don't ditch it just yet.

4. Add in 6 or 8 rows of plain weave in the warp yarn at the bottom of your loom, just above your place-holder, and then add a row of rya knots (page 58) in your light worsted-weight amber yarn. Each of the 23 rya knots should include 6 strands, each measuring about 24" (61 cm) long (Fig. 4).

Creating a Circular Shape

Creating the appearance of a smooth, circular arc on a gridded structure comes down to creating an optical illusion. It's similar to pixelating your circle. Having a template helps you work around the restrictions of a warp and weft, but you'll also need to do a little bit of counting.

5. Add in about 1" (2.5 cm) of plain weave above your rya knots and then focus on the right side of your design. You'll weave the outside of your design using a diagonal slit weave (page 50) instead of interlocking your weft rows. Mark your center 2 warps with a bit of yarn for reference and then weave back toward the center with the same yarn you used to create your plain weave. But instead of weaving to the center 2 warps, decrease 2 more warps to your right. Weave back to the right selvedge of your warp.

   Weave back to the center again, decreasing by 2 more warps before returning to the right selvedge. This helps create a subtle curve in the bottom of your circle. The next row will only decrease by 1 warp. Decrease by 1 warp 3 more times. Then decrease by 1 warp but weave 4 weft rows. This

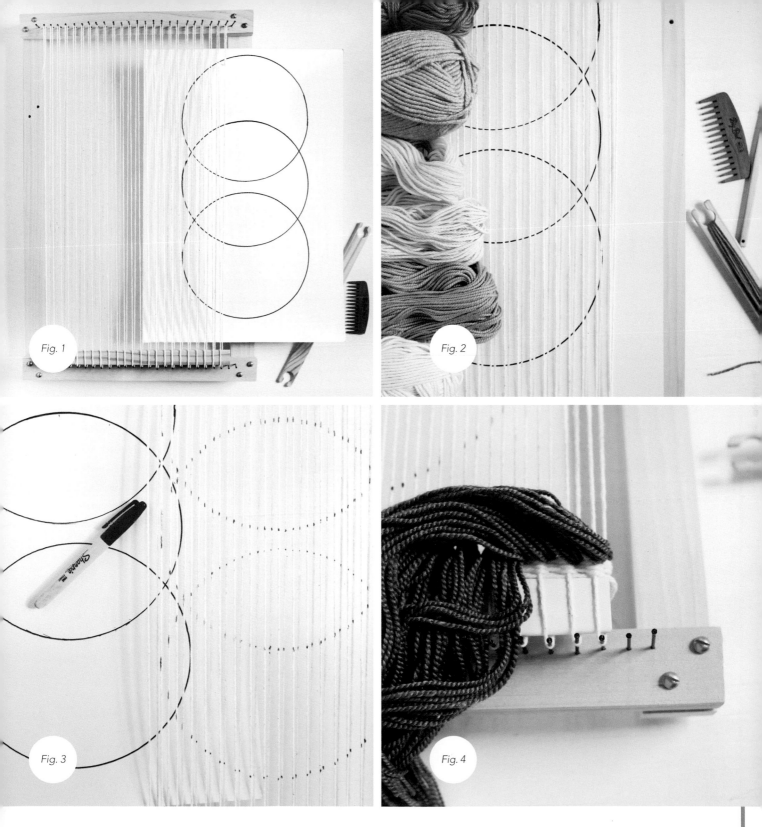

Fig. 1

Fig. 2

Fig. 3

Fig. 4

starts building your curve upward at a higher gradient. Do this 3 more times, continuing to decrease.

Decrease your next warp by 1 and weave 8 weft rows instead of just 4. Do this again.

Next, decrease by 1 warp and weave 12 weft rows. Do this again. You're almost to the outermost edge of the circular shape.

Finally, decrease by 1 warp and weave 28 weft rows. This will create a straight line (Fig. 5). It'll feel really noncircular, but trust the optical illusion and know that this straight line will do its job.

6 Now you need to work backward to create the top of the curve. Increase by 1 warp and weave 12 weft rows. Do this one more time. Then increase 1 warp and weave 8 weft rows. Next, increase 1 warp but weave only 2 weft rows. This has created the space between the bottom circle and the center circle. Check your template to ensure you're still on track. Continue increasing and decreasing your warps according to your template as you work your way up the right side. Then get started on the left-hand side. Mirror your process and use your right side as a count marker as you go (Fig. 6).

If it's a little wonky, don't get discouraged. This isn't a technique that is easily mastered the first time around! You'll learn something each time you attempt it.

7 Filling in your circular shapes is the easy part now! You don't have to build your foundation as much as fill in the blanks with a diagonal slit-weave technique. Use the honey-colored yarn to fill in this bottom color block (Fig. 7). Each weft row should match the weft rows in your outer design as long as the yarns are roughly the same thickness. Be sure to bubble and press down your rows with your comb. This kind of design requires a little more attention so that nothing pulls out of shape.

8 When you get close to creating the curve between your first color and your next color, just follow the template or mimic the same counting you did at the bottom of your first circle. Move your center warp marker up for reference. Continue building your second color block using the mint blue yarn (Fig. 8).

Notice the outer edge of the circle has almost 2" (5 cm) of vertical space between the honey circle and the off-white outer edge. This slit between the 2 color blocks is an example of vertical slit weave. You can create vertical edges between color blocks using this technique, but you wouldn't necessarily want them to be too high, because the slits might pull apart from the weight of your weft rows and create a gap in your design.

One technique used to avoid these slits is a straight interlock technique (page 167). I could've used the straight interlock technique to join the 2 color-block sections, but I would've needed to use the same technique to connect the color blocks along every weft row in order to have a consistent design. This would've taken much longer to weave and would've also blurred the edges where the color blocks meet. While solving one problem, it would've created another. Knowing the limitations of stitches and other options will only increase your abilities to achieve the designs you envision.

9 For your third color block, weave up 1 side and then the other with mint green yarn. Your 2 sides can meet up on the same weft row by overlapping a bit or ending behind the same warp. This will create a seamless line (Fig. 9).

10 Continue weaving your next color block with light peach yarn and then filling in the outer shape with cream yarn as you go (Fig. 10).

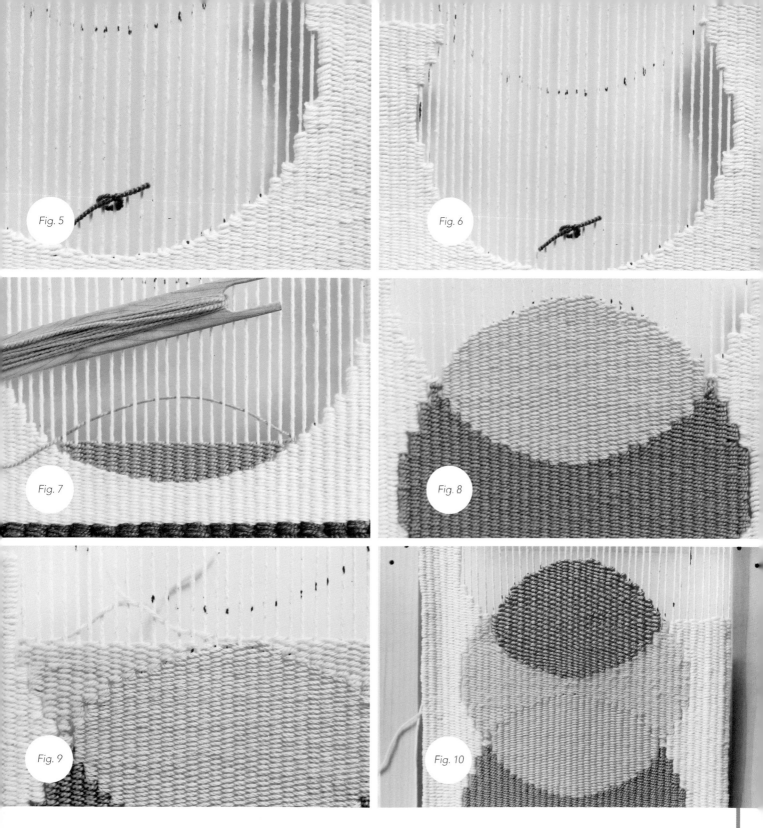

Fig. 5

Fig. 6

Fig. 7

Fig. 8

Fig. 9

Fig. 10

Triple Scoop Wall Hanging | 105

11 Continue working your last 2 color-block sections all the way to the top, using coral and cream yarns. Mimic the same counting at the top of your top circle as you did with the bottom of your bottom circle (Fig. 11). You can see where my template is still acting as a guide even though my circle rests just underneath the marked line.

12 Finish your outer weaving and then add about 1" (2.5 cm) of cream plain weave across the top to give your design some breathing room (Fig. 12).

13 Add a hemstitch (page 50) to finish the top (Fig. 13). If you have just enough space, you can gently remove your warps from each peg at the top and slide a dowel through without having to cut and stitch them through the back of your wall hanging. Either way, add your dowel and a hanger.

14 After you've removed your project from your loom, remove the cardboard placeholder at the bottom and knot off those warp ends to keep the weaving from shifting. If your design has shifted at all after removing it from the loom, gently adjust your weft rows with your fingers to help it regain its shape.

Now that you know how to create rounded edges by increasing weft rows by 1 or 2 warps, you can include circles, ovals, half circles, wavy lines, crescent shapes, scallops, and more in your designs. You can also design cartoons for more intricate patterns. I think you may have just leveled up!

Fig. 11

Fig. 12

Fig. 13

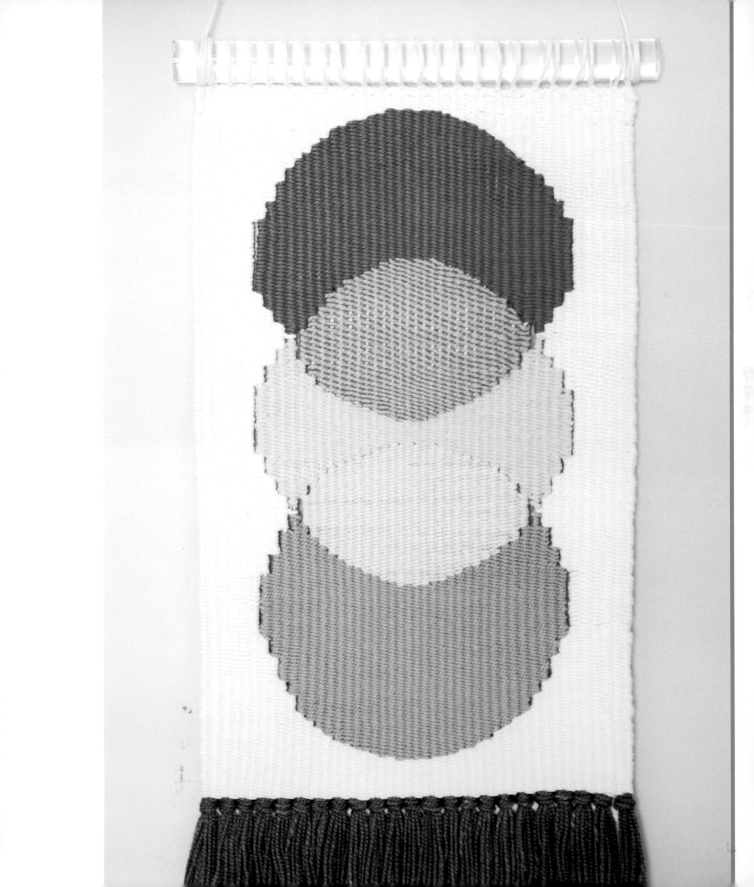

Flighty Wall Hanging

When we lived in Colorado, I attended a forest school group with some other moms where the leader taught the kids how to create makeshift frame looms from sticks. Then we went on a nature walk through the woods to gather materials to weave with. We had scraps of yarn and fabric to fill in the gaps, but we also collected twigs with berries attached, long grasses, wildflowers, and the odd feather shed from a woodpecker or bluebird. It was a beautiful sample of the forest when it was finished, but it also opened my eyes to how many different elements can be woven through a warp to create a beautifully textured piece of art.

This project is asking you to get experimental and look outside the box when it comes to what you use to weave. Instead of a traditional cotton warp, you'll use cotton gima, a fiber that feels a little like paper but is still strong enough for the job. You'll also incorporate dyed feathers, copper pipe, and wool roving that you'll use for fringe instead of as a weft fiber.

Finished Size

13" x 36" (33 x 91.5 cm) including fringe

Supplies

frame loom, 15" x 18" (38 x 45.5 cm)

cotton gima in oak for warp and weft, 60 yards (55 m)

wool roving in mint, 6 yards (5.5 m)

bulky-weight two-ply wool yarn in royal blue, 70 yards (64 m)

20 mint duck feathers

20 royal blue duck feathers

26-gauge jewelry wire, 3 yards (2.75 m)

acrylic dowel, 1" x 12" (2.5 x 30.5 cm)

copper pipe, ¼" x 10" (6 mm x 25.5 cm)

stick shuttle, 8" (20.5 cm)

cardboard placeholder

wooden comb or fork

scissors

small pipe cutter

1 Warp your loom with 26 warps using cotton gima or regular cotton yarn. Be sure to use a shed stick or cardboard placeholder at the bottom. Weave in 10 rows of plain weave to create some structure. Then create shapes by weaving 10 weft rows across the middle 12 warps. Decrease by 2 warps on each side and weave in 10 more weft rows. Repeat again and again until you're just weaving 10 weft rows over the 2 middle warps. This creates a triangle shape.

Increase by 2 warps for every 10 weft rows until you span 12 warps total for a mirrored triangle shape. Then decrease 2 warps, weave 10 weft rows, decrease 2 warps, weave 10 weft rows, and so on until you are just weaving 10 weft rows over the 2 middle warps again (Fig. 1). This will turn that triangle into a diamond.

If you use regular cotton yarn or a thicker wool yarn, you may want to weave only 2 or 4 weft rows instead of 10. Just be consistent in what you choose.

2 Weave in 2 more diamond shapes and end on a triangle shape. Add in 10 more rows of plain weave using the same cotton gima to create some structure at the top of your wall hanging (Fig. 2).

3 Next, create your outer shape by weaving 10 weft rows of cotton gima over the outer 2 warps. Increase 2 warps again and again and then decrease 2 warps. Decrease again to the outer 2 warps, but instead of weaving 10 weft rows, weave 18 or 20 (Fig. 3). Again, if you use cotton yarn or wool, you will want to weave fewer weft rows because you'll have more bulk.

Repeat this process of increasing and decreasing to create half-diamond shapes along the edge of your wall hanging.

4 Repeat the same pattern on the opposite side (Fig. 4). You'll notice your negative space is 2 zigzags.

5 Weave your feathers in so you have 3 or 4 feathers wedged in between each diamond shape (Fig. 5). You may want to play with the angles at the edges to make sure they cover up your negative space.

6 Once your feathers are arranged, cut your pipe into 2" (5 cm) lengths using your small pipe cutter. Thread your first length of pipe with about 6" (15 cm) of jewelry wire (Fig. 6).

Fig. 1

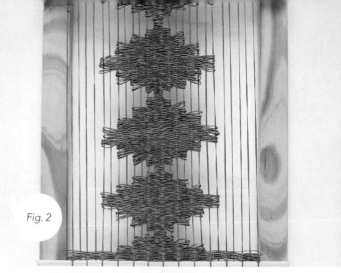

Fig. 2

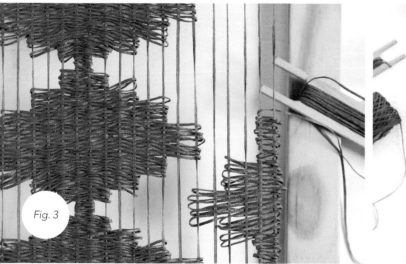

Fig. 3

Fig. 4

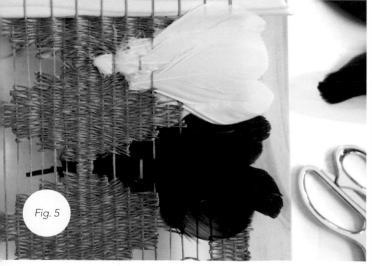

Fig. 5

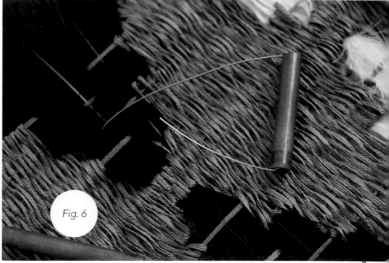

Fig. 6

Fig. 7

Fig. 8

Fig. 9

Fig. 10

7   Pierce through the weft rows in the center of one diamond with the ends of the jewelry wire. Fold the wire to the back of your weaving and twist like you would with a wire bread tie. Trim the ends (Fig. 7). Repeat with the rest of your copper pipe lengths, placing one in the center of each diamond and triangle.

8   Remove the placeholder at the bottom of your loom and spread the plain weave so that there are about 5 rows below and 5 rows above with negative space between. Cut your roving into 9 lengths measuring 18" (45.5 cm) each (Fig. 8).

9   Tie rya knots with the roving, but instead of wrapping the roving around 2 warps right next to each other, leave 1 warp in between the warps you'll be wrapping around. So, there will be 3 warps per rya knot; the exception is the knot on the left edge, which will take only 2 (Fig. 9). Skipping a warp in

between such chunky rya knots gives your roving some wiggle room since the knots are so thick.

10   Cut the royal blue yarn for your next set of rya knots; cut 8 strands measuring 40" (101.5 cm) long for each of 13 knots. Wrap your rya knots around a set of 2 warps as usual, instead of 3 (Fig. 10). Trim your rya knots for even ends. The cotton gima that you pulled down before adding rya knots is acting as the support at the bottom of the wall hanging.

11   Gently remove your weaving from your loom and adjust anything that has shifted. Add your dowel and hanger.

Enjoy your exotic new wall hanging! If you feel so inclined, substitute flowers, that will look equally beautiful when dried, for the feathers or use a cotton warp and strips of cotton fabric for the weft. Add precious stones, beads, or anything else with holes that you can attach with jewelry wire for a custom look.

Milkmaid Braid Wall Hanging

This wall hanging is one of my favorites because it was an experiment that ended up even better than I'd imagined. I'm always eager to find new ways to manipulate a medium, so I decided to adjust my expectations of what a frame loom was and ended up with a cut of leather acting as part of the loom. For interest, I created a triangular shape, but you could easily use a rectangle or semicircle. If you prefer not to use leather, you could substitute thick vinyl or pleather. Just be sure it's something that won't easily rip.

Finished Size

11" x 22" (28 x 56 cm) including fringe

Supplies

frame loom, 12" x 16" (30.5 x 40.5 cm)

pliable leather or thick vinyl, 12" x 5" (30.5 x 12.5 cm)

worsted-weight two-ply cotton yarn in off-white for warp and weft, 75 yards (68.6 m)

worsted-weight single-ply wool in bright red, 15 yards (13.7 m)

worsted-weight single-ply alpaca/wool blend in berry red, 30 yards (27.4 m)

wool roving in mint, 2 yards (1.8 m)

worsted-weight two-ply wool yarn in coral, 80 yards (73.2 m)

wooden dowel, 1" x 12" (2.5 x 30.5 cm)

shed stick, 12" (30.5 cm)

stick shuttle, 8" (20.5 cm)

tapestry needle, 6" (15 cm)

tapestry needle, 2½" (6.5 cm)

leather hole punch or awl

wooden comb or fork

pen

ruler

scissors

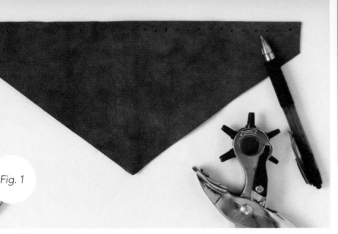

Fig. 1

Fig. 2

1   Measure about 1" (2.5 cm) down from a 12" (30.5 cm) edge of the leather and make a mark on both the right and left sides. Then measure to the center point of the bottom of the leather and make a mark. Connect the side marks and the center mark to form a triangular shape. Cut out the shape (Fig. 1).

2   Use your loom pegs as a template to mark where to punch holes along the long edge of the leather (Fig. 2). Make sure you mark in about ⅜" (1 cm) from the edge of your leather so it doesn't tear.

3   Make a mark for a matching hole straight down from the top row of holes, again keeping the marks about ⅜" (1 cm) in from the edge of the leather. Use a ruler to make sure you are getting mostly straight lines (Fig. 3).

4   Carefully punch your holes with a leather hole punch or awl (Fig. 4).

5   Stitch your leather piece directly to your dowel rod with the off-white cotton yarn (Fig. 5). Tie knots on the back side of the leather at each end of the dowel. Be sure your yarn tension is even across the dowel.

6   Place your dowel just under the top of your loom frame and tie it in 3 places with scrap yarn. You'll cut the scrap yarn off later, but it holds the piece in place for now.

Next, cut the same off-white yarn for your warp and tie a double knot at one end. Thread the unknotted end onto the 2½" (6.5 cm) tapestry needle. Working from the back side of your leather, push the needle through the outer right hole and pull the thread through until you hit the double knot. Then wrap the yarn down around the first nail or peg at the bottom of your frame loom and bring it back up to the second hole from the right. Stitch from the top through to the back of the leather before coming back up through the third hole and back down to the bottom peg (Fig. 6).

Keep this up until you have warped your leather piece to your frame loom. If you run out of warp yarn, end on the back side of your leather with a double knot and start again with another double knot in the next hole before warping the rest. Check that you have even tension and make sure it's taut without pulling too much on the leather. You don't want to stretch it out.

7   Depending on how many holes you've got in your leather, you may end your warp on the top hole of the leather or on the bottom peg of your frame loom (Fig. 7). The hard part is done and now you can get to weaving!

Fig. 3

Fig. 4

Fig. 5

Fig. 6

Fig. 7

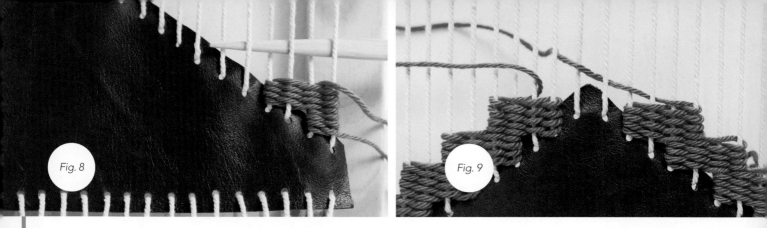

Fig. 8

Fig. 9

8   To more easily weave around the shape of the leather, flip your loom so the leather is on the bottom. With the coral worsted-weight yarn, start weaving a stair-step pattern with 8 weft rows wrapping around the first 2 warps and then increasing 2 warps and weaving in 8 weft rows. Press your rows down just slightly past the edge of the leather for a snug fit (Fig. 8)

9   Shift over to increase and decrease 2 warps every time you make a new stair step of 8 weft rows. Stop before you get to the top stair step and then weave the same pattern on the opposite side of your leather. Weave the tail ends of both sides toward each other (Fig. 9).

10   Overlap your 2 tail ends to create an almost seamless row over the tip of the leather piece (Fig. 10).

11   With a new strand of yarn, continue your stair-step pattern by weaving across 6 warps for 8 weft rows and then reduce by 2 warps on each side and weave another 8 weft rows (Fig. 11).

12   Add 15 rya knots made of 8 strands that measure about 7" (18 cm) long from the bright red worsted-weight yarn to fit on each stair step. These will be turned upside down for a shorter, fuller pile of yarn. To make quicker work of this section, you can just cut

1 length of yarn that measures about 56" (142 cm) and fold it in half 3 times to add your rya knot. Once they are all added, trim your loop ends (Fig. 12).

13   For an even fuller pile, add another layer of rya knots, but stagger them so they don't wrap around the same warps as the first layer (Fig. 13). If you don't stagger the knots, you'll have some spacing between your rows that will separate.

14   Weave in your negative space to the top of your rya knot pile with a slit weave (page 50) using the berry worsted-weight yarn (Fig. 14).

15   Repeat on the opposite side and then continue weaving all the way across to join your berry color block (Fig. 15).

16   Weave in 8 weft rows of berry yarn and then mimic the stair step, slit-weave pattern by decreasing 2 warps and weaving up 8 weft rows on both sides (Fig. 16).

17   Continue the same stair-step pattern until you have 8 weft rows on the middle 2 warps (Fig. 17). Feel free to reorient your loom at this point or keep it upside down, whichever feels more natural.

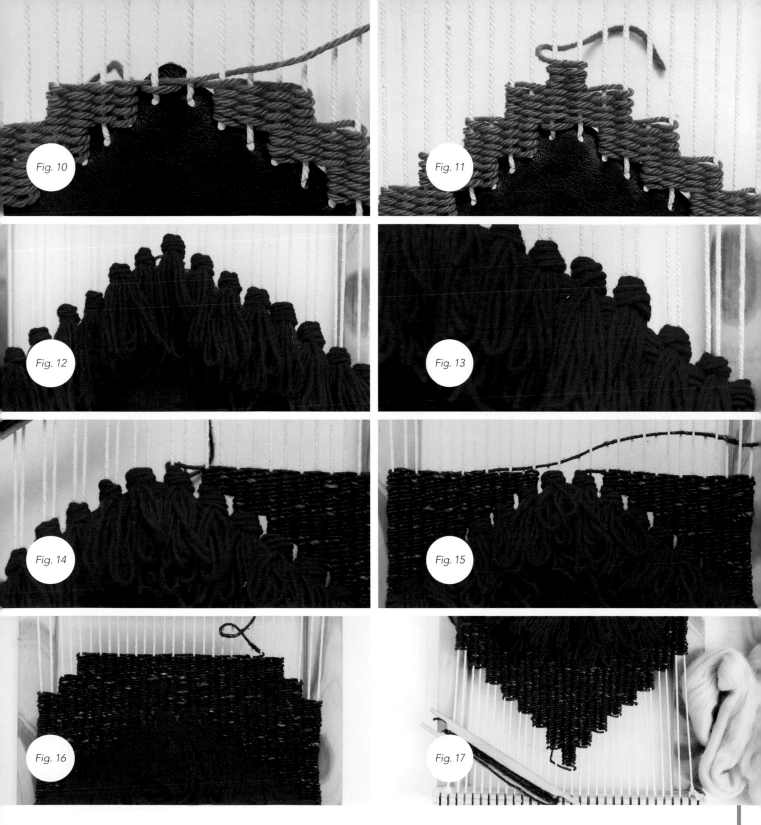

Fig. 10

Fig. 11

Fig. 12

Fig. 13

Fig. 14

Fig. 15

Fig. 16

Fig. 17

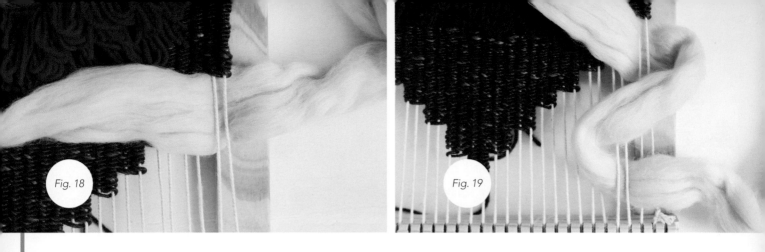

Fig. 18

Fig. 19

18 Tuck one end of your wool roving up between the second and third warps (Fig. 18). You're about to work some soumak magic.

19 Wrap the long end of your roving carefully over 4 warps and back behind 2 warps (Fig. 19). Gently adjust into place. You don't want to pull against the warp as you would with regular wool yarn, as the friction might fray your roving a bit. Just gently lift your warps and make a shed space with one hand as you pull roving through with the other. This takes a little more time but will be worth it for a smoother texture.

20 Continue wrapping over 4 warps and back under 2 (Fig. 20).

21 Adjust your roving as you work your way down (or up) your stair step and gently push it against your last color block (Fig. 21).

22 Wrap your roving around the center 2 warps and then continue your soumak in reverse until you end where you started (Fig. 22). If you run out of roving, simply cut a new length and start where you left off.

23 Repeat on the opposite side and wrap around the same 2 middle warps before returning in the other direction (Fig. 23).

24 Can you see the lovely braided pattern it creates? Such gorgeous texture and depth! Tuck those loose ends under the back of one of your soumak stitches to help them stay in place now or at the end when you're cleaning up the entire back of your weaving (Fig. 24).

Fig. 20

Fig. 22

Fig. 23

Fig. 21

Fig. 24

25 Create a rough stair-step design to fill in the space around the roving using the off-white worsted-weight yarn and more slit weave. Filling in the negative space around roving is a little trickier than around smaller yarns since the roving can be thicker in some weft rows than others, so just focus on filling in the negative space instead of counting how many weft rows you add. Be sure to press each weft row snugly to help lock everything in place.

Add 15 rya knots using the coral yarn. Each of the 12 strands should measure 14" (35.5 cm) long to create more length (Fig. 25).

26 Add another layer of fringe for even more depth by including longer rya knots made from the off-white worsted-weight cotton yarn. Each of the 10 strands should measure about 22" (56 cm) long (Fig. 26).

27 Add in another 6 or 8 rows of plain weave to add some structure to the bottom of your rya knots and then carefully remove your wall hanging from the loom. You can slip the bottom off as usual, but you'll need to cut the 3 pieces of scrap yarn that held your dowel to the top of your frame.

Trim the loops off of your top layer of short bright red rya knots if you haven't already for a fluffy fiber pile and then clean up the back of your wall hanging (Fig. 27). As you can see, one benefit to using a stick shuttle when weaving in large sections of yarn is that you don't have nearly as many tails to stitch back through!

Add a hanger and see how lovely your new wall hanging looks!

Now think of all the other ways you can incorporate non-traditional items into your weavings and other ways you can manipulate your loom. Also, who else wants to create an entire wall hanging with roving in a soumak stitch? I thought so!

Fig. 25

Fig. 26

Fig. 27

Take Me Somewhere Clutch

Even a frame loom of the size we've used thus far can turn out something much more functional than wall art. This project is a simple foldover clutch made from fabric yarn on a cotton warp. I made this clutch in less than an hour thanks to the bulk of the fabric yarn and the simplicity of the design. Despite being grouped in with more complex woven projects, this is a great weaving project for beginners as well as intermediate weavers.

Once you understand how to design around the fold of the clutch, you'll be able to create a variety of patterns, incorporate fringe with rya knots, or customize it by stitching on accessories such as pom-poms or tassels. In the end, you have a one-of-a-kind clutch that will add the perfect amount of excitement to your daily wardrobe.

Finished Size

7½" x 11½" (19 x 29 cm) with a 5" (12.5 cm) flap

Supplies

frame loom, 15" x 18" (38 x 45.5 cm)

worsted-weight two-ply cotton yarn in green-blue for warp, 20 yards (18.3 m)

medium-weight fabric yarn in mustard yellow, 21 yards (19.2 m)

medium-weight fabric yarn in white-and-black, 9 yards (8.2 m)

medium-weight fabric yarn in mint blue, 2 yards (1.8 m)

shed stick, 12" (30.5 cm)

stick shuttle, 8" (20.5 cm)

tapestry needle, 2½" (6.5 cm)

wooden comb or fork

scissors

1   Warp your frame loom with 52 warps using the green-blue worsted-weight yarn. Fabric yarn will create more bulk between weft rows causing your warp to be visible in your design. Choosing a warp cotton in a coordinating color is important because it will need to work with the rest of the colors for the most pleasing outcome. You won't need to use a placeholder in this project since you'll be using all of the space on your warp.

Since you want as few loose ends as possible for this functional piece, cut your fabric yarn into much longer lengths than when you're working on your wall hanging, about 3 yards (2.75 m) each.

Wrapping that much fabric yarn around a stick shuttle will create too much bulk to easily pass through your warp. Instead, wrap the fabric yarn around your stick shuttle twice and pick your way over and under in one direction and then pass through quickly with a shed stick in the other direction.

Begin to plain weave with the mustard fabric yarn (Fig. 1).

2   When you do need to add a new length of yarn, overlap your new tail with the old tail for about 8 warps (Fig. 2).

3   Press the new layer of weft row down on top of the last layer with your comb to secure them in place (Fig. 3).

4   You'll create a seamless line this way, and your ends will be less likely to pull out when locked in with the next weft row (Fig. 4).

5   Weave almost three-quarters of the warp with the mustard yellow for a total of 42 weft rows (Fig. 5). The bottom of the frame will be the inside panel of the clutch, and the top quarter will be the folded-over flap of the clutch.

6   Flip your loom if you prefer for easier access to this end or just to help as you design the flap of the clutch. Decrease 1 warp for every 2 weft rows of white-and-black fabric yarn until you fill your warp space or reach 18 weft rows (Fig. 6). Continue to bubble as you weave each row to avoid your warp edges pulling into an hourglass shape.

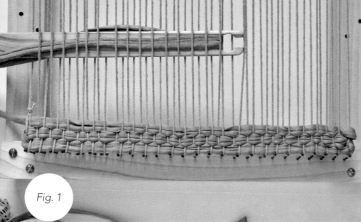

Fig. 1

Fig. 2

Fig. 3

Fig. 4

Fig. 5

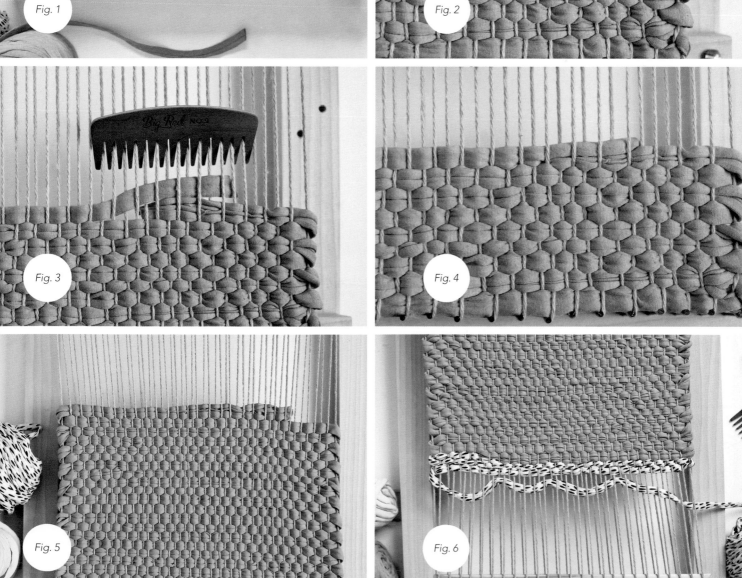

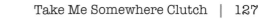

Fig. 6

Fig. 7

Fig. 8

7 Start the mint blue fabric yarn by interlocking through the top selvedge edge of white-and-black fabric yarn. Tuck your tail end down between the first and second warps (Fig. 7).

8 Wrap your long end around the outer warp and through the next loop of white-and-black yarn (Fig. 8). This will start your diagonal interlock (pages 86–88). Ideally, you'll weave through either the back side or the front of each loop no matter which direction they favor for a flatter weave. If you forget and loop through the back side on one and the front on the next, it's not the end of the world.

9 Continue by wrapping your mint blue yarn under the outer warp (Fig. 9).

10 Weave up and around that outer warp and under the second warp before interlocking with the white-and-black loop (Fig. 10). You can see here I went through the front side instead of the back side. I won't tell if you don't!

11 Continue weaving over and under as you regularly would, but interlock with each white-and-black loop instead of just resting next to it (Fig. 11). This diagonal interlock technique avoids awkward spaces on a functional design and helps to reinforce the structure.

12 Weave this section for 5"–6" (12.5–15 cm) until you're happy with the length (Fig. 12).

13 Gently pull the weaving off the loom and tie warp knots flush against the last weft row (Fig. 13).

14 Flip your clutch over and stitch in the tails of the mint blue and white-and-black fabric yarn sections (Fig. 14).

Fig. 9

Fig. 10

Fig. 11

Fig. 12

Fig. 13

Fig. 14

15 As you can see, there are small bits of ends that will stick out (Fig. 15). That's fine since fabric yarn won't ravel and turn into a mess with use.

16 Fold your clutch into thirds and trim the loop ends off of your warp fringe (Fig. 16). If you prefer, you can weave the warp back in the underside or design your clutch so that this is the inside panel of your clutch instead of the flap because the inside panel on this clutch is flush with the other end of the warp loops.

17 Next, you will stitch the edges together with more fabric yarn in the same color as the body so that it's almost seamless. To start, thread the tapestry needle with mustard fabric yarn. With the clutch body folded, stitch from under the bottom loop on the front side so that you're on the inside of the warp as well (Fig. 17).

18 Tie a double knot and then open your clutch up. Stitch your needle through the looped row just underneath the knot so that you're interlocking around the outer warp (Fig. 18).

19 Fold your clutch again so you can match the next looped row and continue stitching back and forth like you're lacing a shoe. Gently pull your yarn taut every few rows to be sure the 2 sections of the clutch are matching up (Fig. 19).

20 Continue stitching to the top of the inside panel and back through the next looped row on the back of the clutch (Fig. 20).

Fig. 15

Fig. 16

Fig. 17

Fig. 18

Fig. 19

Fig. 20

21 Pull your yarn taut and lace down through so you end up stitching back down into the clutch (Fig. 21). Tie a knot and trim your yarn.

22 This is how your edge should look (Fig. 22). Repeat on the opposite side.

23 When you're finished stitching the sides, the inside of your clutch will look like this (Fig. 23). You can see fabric yarn provides a lot of structure, but it's also wonderfully pliable.

Go the extra mile and attach a hand strap or cross-body strap made from braided fabric yarn. Or add tassels or pom-poms across the front flap for a little more flair. Create one on a larger, custom loom and turn it into a soft tote or messenger bag. Experiment with smaller cotton and wool fibers or even paracord for a completely different texture and aesthetic!

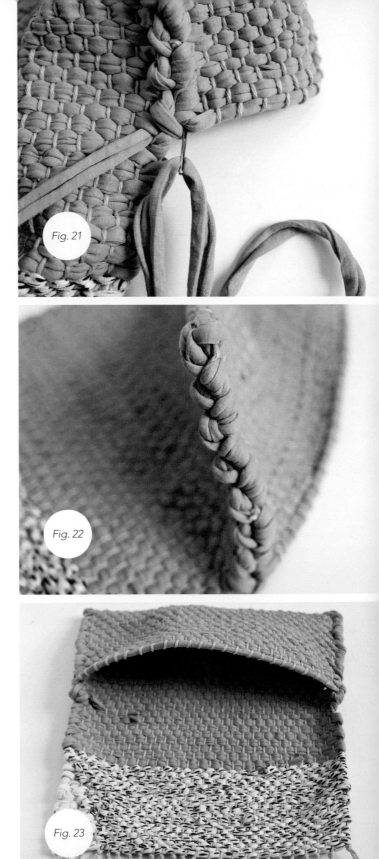

Fig. 21

Fig. 22

Fig. 23

Indigo Dreams Table Runner

Your large 4' x 6' (1.2 x 1.8 m) loom is the perfect height for this next project, a graphic table runner with hints of a traditional border found in both Turkish and Navajo woven rugs. It's a simple but repetitive design that can be made in a few afternoon or evening sessions listening to your favorite podcasts or watching reality TV. The end result is an heirloom piece you can display in your own space or gift to someone special that appreciates the magic of something handmade.

I used an incredible indigo hand-dyed, worsted-weight yarn that reminds me of shibori, a Japanese binding technique that produces beautifully dyed patterns. Paired with a natural-wool yarn, this style is feeling very hippy, homesteader to me. I'm all about that! I can also see this pattern or something similar being woven in a high-contrast black and white for another neutral option.

Finished Size

10" x 64" (25.5 x 162.5 cm) including fringe

Supplies

frame loom, 4' x 6' (1.2 x 1.8 m)

worsted-weight two-ply cotton yarn in cream for warp, 70 yards (64 m)

worsted-weight two-ply wool yarn in indigo, 40 yards (36.6 m)

bulky-weight two-ply wool yarn in cream, 70 yards (64 m)

shed stick, 12" (30.5 cm)

stick shuttles, 6" (15 cm)

tapestry needle, 6" (15 cm)

tapestry needle, 3" (7.5 cm)

scissors

1   Warp your loom with the cream worsted-weight cotton yarn. Start with a loop knot at the top and then wrap your yarn up and down across your nail heads so that you end with another loop knot 18 nail heads across from where you started at the top (Fig. 1). Check that your tension is even by plucking at the warp. If it feels too loose, weave a ½" (1.3 cm) dowel through your warp and let it rest at the bottom near your nail heads. If it's still too loose, you may want to work to tighten 1 warp at a time. Cut off your extra length and tie a new knot.

2   Wrap your stick shuttles with the indigo border yarn. I suggest 2 stick shuttles so you can work your way up each side at the same time to help keep your count and your tension even. Leave about 4" (10 cm) of space from the nail heads and then weave 10 rows of plain weave all the way across your warp using the indigo yarn.

To create this half-triangle pattern, increase 1 warp every 4 weft rows on each side. Once you get 8 warps from the selvedge, start your next weft row by weaving around the warp and then go back to the selvedge. That's the start of your next half triangle. Weave about 4 half triangles on each side (Fig. 2).

3   Now fill in the negative space with your cream yarn. Thread the cream bulky wool yarn on the 6" (15 cm) tapestry needle. The bulky yarn needs only 2 weft rows per increase or decrease in warp. Use the diagonal slit-weave technique (page 50) to fill in the negative space for a strong contrasting line between the 2 color blocks (Fig. 3). An interlock would take you ages, and this type of half-triangle design leaves very small slits between color blocks. An interlock might be preferable only if you want a tightly woven, dovetail effect between the lines of the 2 color blocks.

4   Continue working your way up your warp in sections (Fig. 4). I suggest weaving the border and the negative space up the warp together every 4 half-triangle shapes or so to help keep your tension and design consistent.

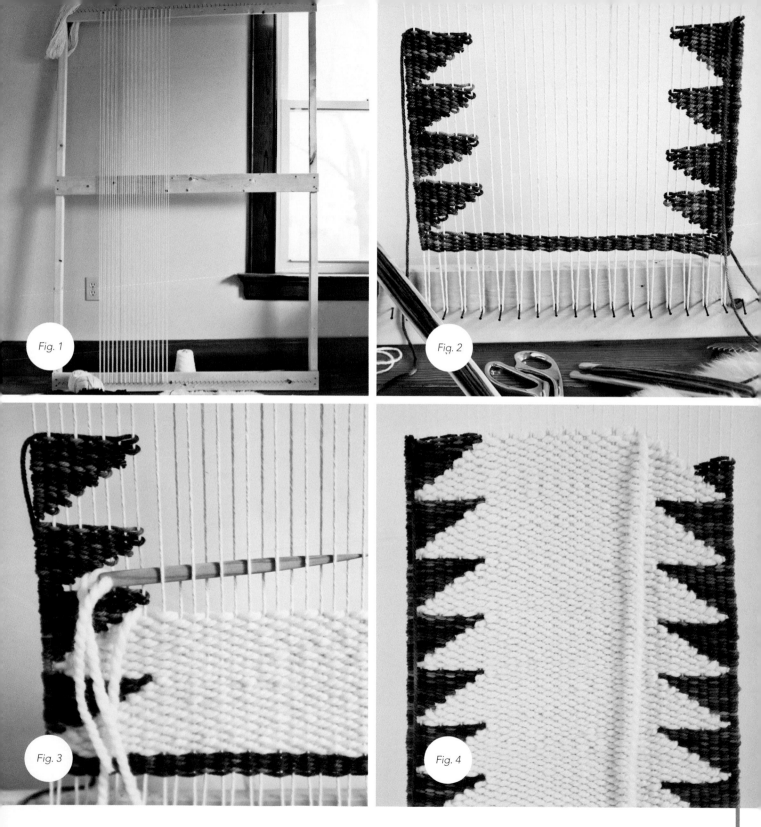

Fig. 1

Fig. 2

Fig. 3

Fig. 4

Indigo Dreams Table Runner | 137

5   Turn the sixteenth half triangle into a full triangle and then switch the direction of the rest of the half triangles so they mirror the bottom half of the design (Fig. 5).

6   I suggest stepping back about 5' (1.5 m) from your work every now and then to make sure you can clearly see if your half triangles are lining up on both sides (Fig. 6). I got back in the habit of weaving half triangles the wrong direction twice and had to pull my progress out and start over.

7   Weave the same number of half triangles from the center before adding in 10 more rows of plain weave (Fig. 7). Carefully pull your top loops off of the nail heads and tie each in a knot to secure the weaving. Repeat with the bottom warp loops. Trim the loops off for a fringe; tuck them back, and stitch them in for a clean edge; or attach tassels or pom-poms to the edges for an even more interesting look.

For a more whimsical design, use long lengths of leftover yarn from other projects for the side triangles. You can weave in the ends at the back of the piece or just leave the back messy.

Fig. 5

Fig. 6

Fig. 7

Fringe Benefits Pillow Sham

A cozy couch or bed can never have too many beautiful pillows! Did you know you can weave those, too? Your large frame loom obviously wants to earn its keep by making itself useful for so many more things than just rugs! This design incorporates simple plain weave as well as chunky rya knots, so you know it's not too complicated of a project. In the end, you get these fantastic pillows that will make you want to brew some coffee and grab a good book for an afternoon of self-care. The supply list is for one pillow, so be sure to double it for a set of pillows.

Finished Size

15" x 15" (38 x 38 cm) pillow

Supplies Per Pillow

frame loom, 4' x 6' (1.2 x 1.8 m)

worsted-weight cotton/alpaca blend yarn in gray for warp, 76 yards (69.5 m)

bulky-weight single-ply wool yarn in camel, 15 yards (13.7 m)

bulky-weight two-ply wool yarn in cream, 70 yards (64 m)

bulky-weight single-ply wool yarn in ochre, 8 yards (7.3 m)

worsted-weight two-ply wool yarn in orange, 6 yards (5.5 m)

worsted-weight two-ply cotton yarn in cream, 4 yards (3.7 m)

printed cotton fabric, 17" x 17" (43 x 43 cm)

natural white cotton fabric, 17" x 17" (43 x 43 cm)

polyester stuffing for pillows

wooden dowel, ¼" x 24" (6 mm x 61 cm)

shed stick, 12" (30.5 cm)

stick shuttle, 12" (30.5 cm)

tapestry needle, 6" (15 cm)

tapestry needle, 2½" (6.5 cm)

cardboard placeholder, 2" x 20" (5 x 51 cm)

wooden comb or fork

sewing machine

cotton thread

straight pins

scissors

1. Did you know you can weave around a frame without any pegs or nails? It's the most basic version of frame-loom weaving. Since we need a little less height than the top of the 4' x 6' (1.2 x 1.8 m) loom, you're going to wrap your warp around the center piece of wood on your loom. Using the worsted-weight gray yarn, tie a loop knot at the bottom nail head and then wrap your warp over the wood from front to back before wrapping it around your next nail head and back over the wood. Continue wrapping over the wood in a consistent manner until you have a warp that is about 4" (10 cm) wider than you want your pillow. This allows for a little shrinkage as you weave as well as when you stitch it up.

   Since the thickness of the wood creates a large gap between the warps, weave the dowel (or a yardstick) through your warp (Fig. 1). This will help close that gap and create a flatter plane on which you can weave. This is in place of weaving 4 or 6 rows of plain weave across your warp to help bring them to a central point and create a flatter surface plane. If you were to weave with a frame loom without any nails or pegs, you'd add rows of plain weave to one or both ends of your warp to help flatten out your warp.

2. Place the cardboard placeholder at the bottom of your warp and add about 1" (2.5 cm) of plain weave using the cream worsted cotton yarn (Fig. 2). This creates a dense patch of weaving to sew through later.

3. Create 1"–2" (2.5–5 cm) of plain weave using the camel bulky wool yarn (Fig. 3).

4. Build up a stair-step pattern on both sides by leaving the center 2 warps alone and weaving up 2 weft rows before decreasing 2 warps. Continue until you get to the outer 2 warps and then repeat the process on the other side (Fig. 4).

5. Cut rya knots from the ochre bulky yarn. If you'd like to add more dimension to your fringe, include a more textured yarn in the same or a similar tone. Each rya knot contains about 6 strands that measure about 5" (12.5 cm) long, and you'll make 21 knots for this row. Wrap the strands around 2 warps and follow the stair-step pattern, but don't add one to the outer 2 warps (Fig. 5). That will be stitched over in a later step.

6. Fill in the negative space between the rya knots with a diagonal slit weave (page 50) using the cream bulky yarn (Fig. 6). Since this is a bulky yarn, you'll easily match the same amount of weft rows as the other bulky yarn used earlier. Weave plain weave until you're about 2" (5 cm) from the top rya knots.

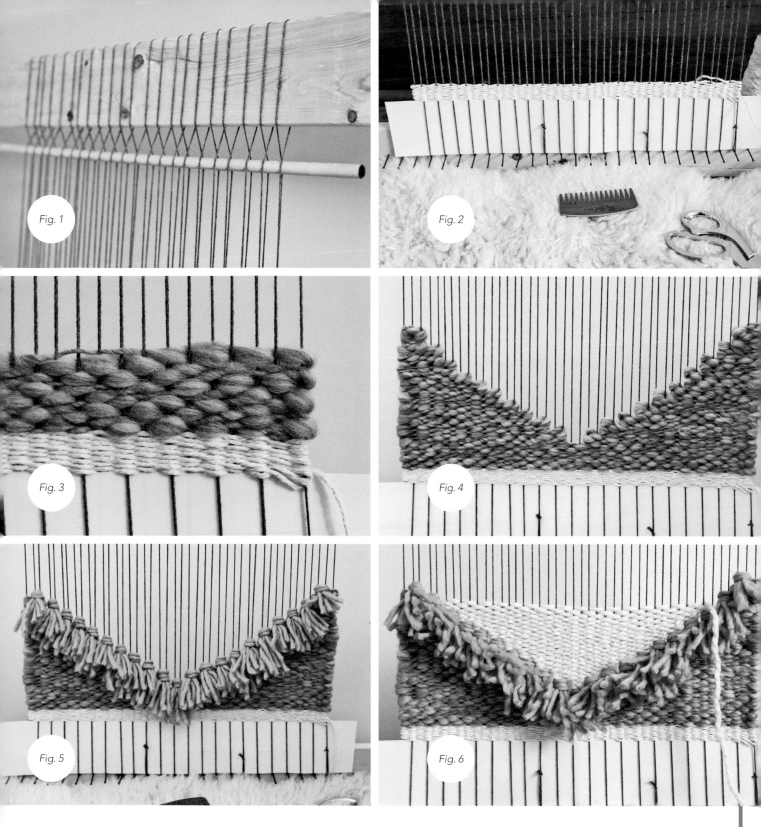

Fig. 1

Fig. 2

Fig. 3

Fig. 4

Fig. 5

Fig. 6

7 Place a rya knot to act as a marker around the center 2 warps (Fig. 7) and continue filling in with the same stair-step pattern as you did below your first set of rya knots: 2 weft rows up and then decrease by 2 warps until you get to the edge. Repeat on the opposite side.

8 Fill in another row of rya knots and then repeat the same process one more time to get a third set of rya knots. Fill in the negative space above your third set of rya knots and then add another 3" (7.5 cm) of plain weave with more cream bulky yarn. Top it off with 1" (2.5 cm) of plain weave with the cream worsted-weight cotton yarn to help secure the weaving at the top where you'll be sewing.

Gently cut the top strands of your pillow top so that you have enough length to tie a knot snugly against your last woven row. Don't worry about trimming the strands because they'll get stitched inside the pillow. Gently pull your pillow top off the bottom row of nail heads, remove your placeholder, and tie up your warp knots (Fig. 8). Ta-da! You've finished a pillow top!

9 Gather your sewing supplies as listed previously (Fig. 9). You could attempt to handstitch this, but it may be harder to achieve a polished end result unless you're experienced with stitching together bulky layers.

10 Place your solid fabric down and then place your printed fabric on top of it with the right side facing you. Place your pillow top with the right side down on top of your printed fabric. It's a pillow sandwich. Pin your pillow top and fabric layers together with straight pins so nothing budges when you stitch it together (Fig. 10).

11 Carefully stitch along the perimeter of your pillow top about ¼" (6 mm) from the edge (Fig. 11). Also make sure you are stitching somewhere between the first and second warps when you stitch along the sides. Leave a 5" (12.5 cm) space between where you start sewing and where you stop so you can turn your pillow right side out.

12 Remove your straight pins and trim off the corners of the fabric as shown. Leave the corners of the weaving intact to help ensure your woven pillow top doesn't get pulled apart. Trim off any excess fabric around the perimeter of the weaving (Fig. 12).

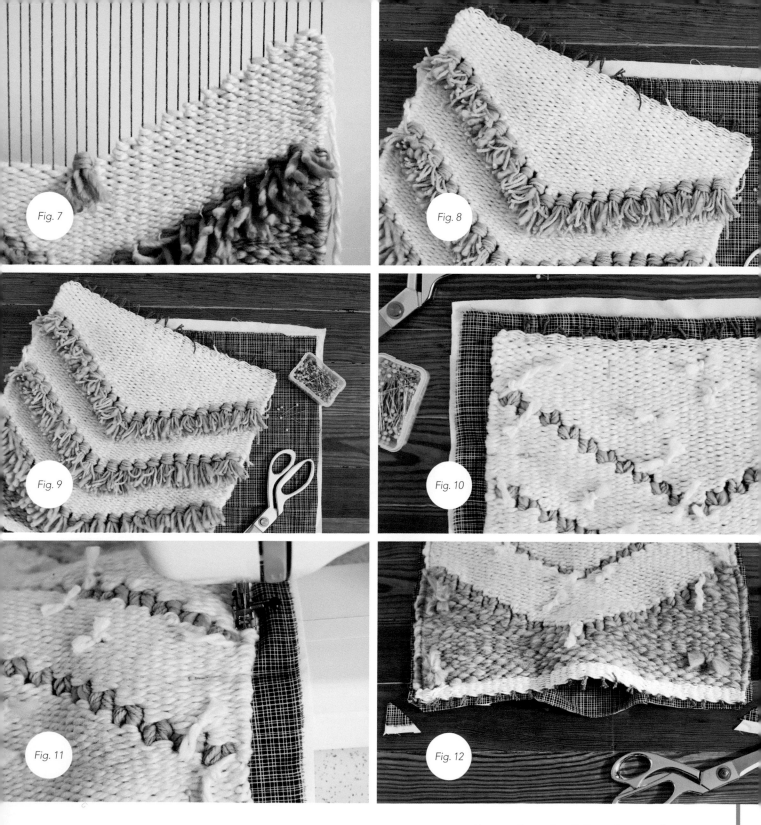

Fig. 7

Fig. 8

Fig. 9

Fig. 10

Fig. 11

Fig. 12

13 Carefully turn your pillow right side out and insert stuffing between the solid and printed layers of fabric (Fig. 13). The solid layer will help prevent any stuffing from working its way out through a random slit in your weaving.

14 Once you're happy with the amount of stuffing inside, carefully pin your opening shut with straight pins and machine stitch your layers together (Fig. 14). You can handstitch this closed with a blind stitch for an almost invisible seam, but sometimes a girl has got to get on with her day!

Throw your new pillow on your bed and take a nap. You deserve it.

Fig. 13

Fig. 14

Last Summer Statement Wall Hanging

If you're looking to make something epic, this is the project for you. This is a wall hanging that commands attention but also feels a little calming. It's the perfect piece to place on a large wall or over a high mantel. Customize your own to fit your specific aesthetic or make one as a gift for a friend. There are so many different stitches, techniques, and fibers that come together in this abstract design to create movement and interest, and the best part is, there aren't a lot of rules or counting involved. You finally get to weave in peace!

Finished Size

31" x 40" (79 x 101.5 cm)

Supplies

frame loom, 4' x 6' (1.2 x 1.8 m)

worsted-weight two-ply cotton yarn in natural for warp, weft, and fringe, 50 yards (45.7 m)

wool roving in natural, 2½ yards (2.3 m)

worsted-weight two-ply wool yarn in off-white, 40 yards (36.6 m)

worsted-weight two-ply polyester yarn in off-white, 60 yards (55 m)

bulky-weight single-ply wool yarn in teal, 13 yards (12 m)

bulky-weight two-ply polyester yarn in cream, 60 yards (55 m)

bulky-weight single-ply wool yarn in natural, 30 yards (27.4 m)

light worsted-weight two-ply wool yarn in peach, 100 yards (91.4 m)

bulky-weight single-ply wool yarn in camel, 25 yards (22.9 m)

bulky-weight single-ply wool yarn in pink, 5 yards (4.6 m)

cotton gima in oak, 2 yards (1.8 m)

worsted-weight single-ply alpaca/wool blend yarn in dark olive, 5 yards (4.6 m)

fingering-weight dyed linen yarn in indigo, 200 yards (182.8 m)

brass square tube, 1" x 36" (2.5 x 91.5 cm)

⅜" (1 cm) cotton rope, 3 yards (2.75 m)

wooden dowel, ¼" x 36" (6 mm x 91.5 cm)

2 yardsticks to use as a shed stick and a placeholder

stick shuttle, 12" (30.5 cm)

tapestry needle, 6" (15 cm)

tapestry needle, 2½" (6.5 cm)

wooden comb or fork

scissors

1 The first step to an epic wall hanging is warping your loom. You'll use your custom 4' x 6' (1.2 x 1.8 m) loom for this, but you'll wrap the top of your warp over the support beam in the center of your frame. Wrap 88 warps using the natural worsted-weight cotton yarn. Check that your tension is evenly distributed all the way across your warp by weaving your 36" (91.5 cm) wooden dowel through and pushing it toward the top of your loom. Keep it in place to help bring your warp together.

Next, weave your yardstick over and under your warp so that it spans the width of your warp. This will act as your shed stick and make quicker work of weaving in one direction. You'll pull it down when you want to create a shed to slide your stick shuttle through in one direction and then push it back up and out of the way when you weave back in the other direction. I suggest weaving in a second yardstick as a placeholder at the bottom of your warp.

2 Weave 6 rows of plain weave using the warp yarn. Starting on the left side of your warp, attach 1 rya knot with about 25 strands that measure about 20" (51 cm) long cut from the off-white polyester yarn. Gently adjust the knot so that all of the strands are running horizontally without a lot of overlap for a more finished look. This takes a little more care since you're using so many strands.

3 Add your second rya knot from the same polyester yarn but make the 25 strands measure 24" (61 cm) long. Add 5 more rya knots with 25 strands each from the same polyester yarn, cutting your strands to measure 30" (76 cm) long. If you run out of polyester yarn before you finish your last knot, add in some strands from another skein of yarn in off-white or natural. This fringe was designed to have a lot of texture by including different thicknesses and types of fiber in some of the rya knots.

Create a finger-knit garland (page 152) measuring about 40" (101.5 cm) for your next rya knot. You'll weave 2 more finger-knit garlands in the body of your weaving, so feel free to make them all now if you prefer.

Quick Rya Knots

A quick way to cut even strands for rya knots is to wrap your yarn around something the size you prefer, such as a flattened cardboard box. Once you have enough strands wrapped around, cut along one edge of your yarn loops and count them out as you create your rya knots.

Fig. 1

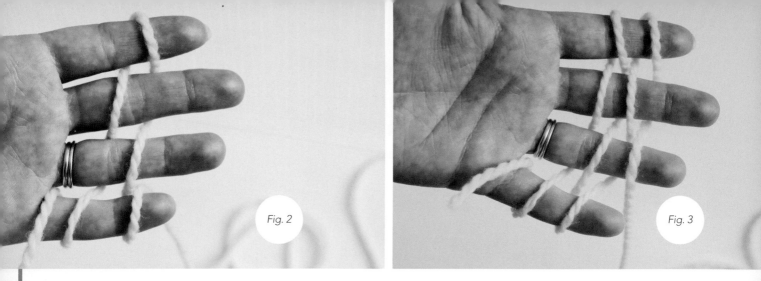

Fig. 2

Fig. 3

Finger Knitting

4 To create a finger-knit garland, leave the tail of yarn between your ring and pinky fingers and wrap back up and around your pinky finger. Wrap it under your ring finger, over your middle finger, under your index finger, and then back in the opposite direction so that it loops back around your pinky finger (Fig. 2).

5 Weave in the direction of your index finger and back again toward your pinky finger stopping just short of your pinky (Fig. 3).

6 Grab the first weft row on your pinky finger and pull it up and over the top of your finger so that it rests on the back of your finger. Repeat with the first weft row on your ring finger (Fig. 4).

7 Continue with the first weft row on your middle finger (Fig. 5).

8 Finally, do the same with the first weft row on your index finger. This is what it will look like on the back side of your fingers for this step (Fig. 6).

9 Take the long end of your yarn and weave it around the back side of your pinky finger and under your ring finger. Continue weaving toward your index finger and then back in the other direction. Stop just short of your pinky finger again.
   Repeat the process of folding the bottom weft row over the top of your finger for all four fingers (Fig. 7).

10 After you've done this about 4 times, pull snugly on the tail of yarn until it forms a knot (Fig. 8). This will also help you see how the loops are starting to form a garland.

11 Continue the process of adding a new top weft row and then folding over the bottom weft row until you've either run out of yarn or have the length you'd like. Tie your other loose end through all 4 remaining loops on your fingers and form a knot (Fig. 9). This is a great project to do while listening to a podcast or watching a movie, as it's almost mindless once you get into a rhythmic pattern. In the end, you'll have a lovely chunky garland to add into your large wall hanging as a fringe or as weft yarn.

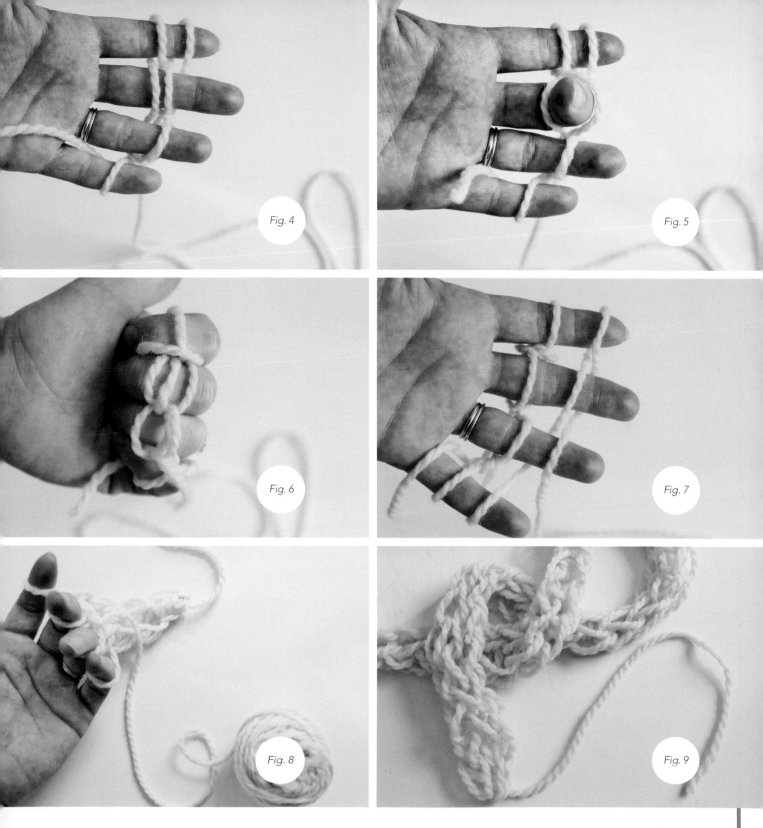

Fig. 4

Fig. 5

Fig. 6

Fig. 7

Fig. 8

Fig. 9

Last Summer Statement Wall Hanging | 153

Create 23 more rya knots made from about 25 strands that each measure about 30" (76 cm) long using polyester yarn. Add in a single strand of bulky wool yarn to a few of those to add texture and interest if you prefer. Next, add in 10 rya knots made from the cream bulky polyester yarn that contain about 25 strands that measure 40" (101.5 cm) each. Mix up your next rya knot with a combination of worsted-weight cotton yarn and bulky polyester yarn with 25 strands that measure about 40". Add in your last 2 rya knots made entirely of worsted-weight cotton yarn using 25 strands that measure about 24" (61 cm) long. This should complete your row of rya knots. Trim the last rya knot to be 2" (5 cm) shorter than the one next to it.

12 Add another 1" (2.5 cm) of plain weave above your row of rya knots to provide some dense structure with 2-ply cotton yarn in natural. Then add in 1 weft row of cream bulky polyester yarn that reaches about 60 warps across. Reduce each additional weft row by 1 warp until you've completed 13 weft rows (Fig. 10). A 12" (30.5 cm) stick shuttle will be your best friend on a larger project like this, so be sure to use it.

13 Create 24' (7.3 m) of finger-knit garland to weave in on the bottom right side of your warp to fill in the negative space. Weave up to the same weft row as the previous color block and then add another 2 weft rows and increase 1 warp so that it overlaps that color block. Then decrease 1 warp for every 2 weft rows 5 more times. This will create an arrow shape and is an example of diagonal slit weave (page 50).

14 Just above the top left corner of the finger-knit garland, add in 2 rya knots with about 9 strands of bulky teal yarn that each measure about 20" (51 cm) long. Add in 3 rya knots with about 60 strands that each measure 24" (61 cm) long using the indigo fingering-weight linen yarn (Fig. 11).

15 Just above your first color block, weave in 1 strand of pink bulky wool yarn that starts about 10 warps in from the left side and fills in the negative space on that weft row. Tuck the tails to the back side as usual. Next, weave in 1 bundle of peach yarn made up of 15 strands that each measure 40" (101.5 cm) long so that it's woven directly above the pink yarn. Be sure to leave about 13" (33 cm) of loose strands hanging through the front side as shown (Fig. 12). This is an easy way to incorporate vertical patterns in your design like you would with a rya knot.

Fig. 10

Fig. 11

Fig. 12

16 Fill in the space next to your bundle of peach yarns with off-white worsted-weight wool yarn and then weave about 1" (2.5 cm) of plain weave above it. Continue to fill in the negative space. Add in a length of pink yarn 6 warps in from the left side and end after the forty-sixth weft row with the tail tucked to the back of the warp. Directly above it, weave in another bundle of peach yarns made up of 15 strands that each measure 40" (101.5 cm) long with the loose strands hanging through the front again. Fill in more negative space around and above this bundle of yarns with more of the off-white worsted-weight wool yarn. Add another strand of pink yarn starting with the eighth warp from the left and ending at the forty-ninth warp. Include one last bundle of peach strands in the same manner as the previous two (Fig. 13).

17 Create another 5 yards (4.6 m) of finger-knit garland using the off-white worsted-weight wool yarn. Start by filling in the negative space around the bundle of peach strands and then weave across a few weft rows to fill in the negative space next to the teal rya knot. Decrease about 7 warps from where the rya knots were, weave 2 weft rows, decrease about 14 warps, weave 2 more weft rows, and then decrease warps in smaller amounts until you have a total of 12 weft rows of finger-knit garland (Fig. 13). This will take up a considerable chunk of warp space in a short amount of time and create a great amount of texture.

18 Create a color block of camel heather yarn around the rya knots (Fig. 13). Shift warps back and forth on both sides for a total of 48 weft rows high. Just to the right of that, fill in the negative space with a bundle of 5 strands of worsted-weight peach yarn for 4 weft rows. Add in 4 weft rows of pink and then weave 5 more weft rows of bundled peach yarn.

19 Fill in the spaces in between the garland and camel yarn with a color block of dark olive worsted-weight yarn measuring about 32 weft rows high. Above this weave a color block of natural worsted-weight cotton yarn measuring about 34 weft rows high. Just above that on the left side, weave a color block that includes 16 weft rows of finger-knit garland using polyester yarn in cream in a stair-step pattern. Just to the right of that, weave a color block with 12 weft rows of off-white bulky polyester yarn. To the right of that, weave a color block with 26 weft rows of off-white worsted-weight wool yarn.

20 Make some room for those roving soumak stitches! Since this roving is so thick, weave over 4 warps and back 1 warp starting just right of the center of your warp and filling in the negative space on the left side of that weft row (Fig. 14).

21 Weave more soumak back in the direction you came for a lovely herringbone or braided effect, but decrease by 8 warps before weaving back to the left (Fig. 15).

22 Add in another layer of soumak to fill in some more space and to get a shape similar to the rest of the color block shapes. Tuck your tail to the back (Fig. 16).

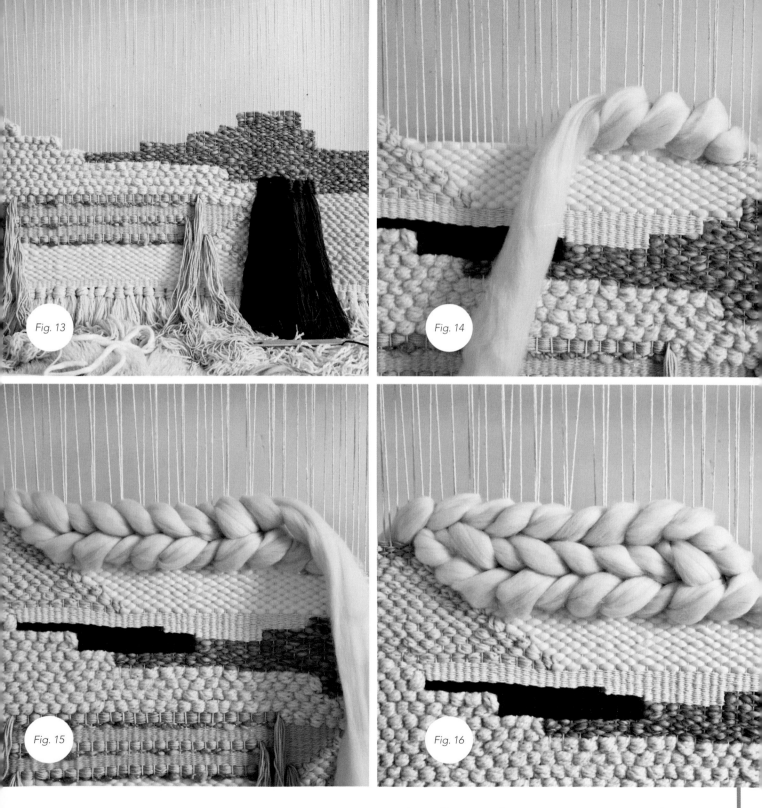

Fig. 13

Fig. 14

Fig. 15

Fig. 16

23 If your warp is a little out of whack directly above your roving soumak, add in plain weave with the bulky polyester yarn to even out those threads and provide a little stability (Fig. 17). Fill in the left side with a bundle of 4 strands of peach yarn for 4 weft rows.

24 Move to the right side of your warp and add 3 weft rows of cream bulky polyester yarn before weaving in a thick bundle of off-white worsted-weight wool yarn. This will include about 50 strands and will fill in the negative space to the right of the wool roving for 4 weft rows. Add 4 rows of plain weave just above this space with oak cotton gima and then add 8 rows of plain weave using the bulky polyester yarn all the way across the width of your warp.

25 Finish off your wall hanging with the hemstitch and then a knot, as the weight of this beautiful monster might need that extra support. Stitch your wall hanging around a brass tube (Fig. 18) or something both strong and interesting like a poplar branch, 1" (2.5 cm) wooden dowel, or acrylic rod. Trim your bottom row of rya knots at interesting angles or cut it evenly across the bottom. Add a hanger and find a place to show off this large weaving!

Fig. 17

Fig. 18

Positive Vibes Rug

Weaving your own rug might seem a little ambitious, but if I can do it, you can do it. This design is a little more complex than the first rug I ever wove, but it's just a giant star motif, similar to The Stars at Night on page 78. You can easily alter this pattern and weave bold stripes similar to I Want Candy on page 34 if you'd rather work on something without diagonal lines. If a large rug just feels too intimidating, use the center board as the top part of your loom and weave a bath-sized rug instead.

Fabric yarn is an excellent choice for weaving a rug because it can be found in a variety of colors and patterns, it's quite durable, and it's thick enough to make quicker work than if you were using a worsted-weight wool yarn. It has a lovely weight and drape to it, so it isn't easily disturbed when walked across. But you will still need to pair it with a rug pad if you use it on hardwood or tiled floors.

Most of the fabric yarns I used here are fashion industry remnants that have been cut and wound into balls of yarn. Many of these are a cotton blend, but the fettuccia yarn is a little more like rayon. *Fettuccia* is Italian for ribbon or strip and is currently a fashionable yarn to use in Europe. When using fabric yarns made of different fibers and with different elasticity, be doubly aware that you aren't pulling your weft rows taut as you weave to ensure everything lies flat when you remove it from the loom.

This rug is machine washable, but I suggest spot cleaning instead. Vacuum over it as you would with regular rugs.

Finished Size

3' x 5½' (91.5 cm x 1.7 m)

Supplies

frame loom, 4' x 6' (1.2 x 1.8 m)

⅜" (1 cm) cotton rope in natural for warp, 384 yards (351 m)

11 oz. fettuccia yarn in olive green, 140 yards (128 m)

medium fabric yarn in light pink, 140 yards (128 m)

medium fabric yarn in pink, 140 yards (128 m)

medium fabric yarn in light mint, 140 yards (128 m)

medium fabric yarn in ochre, 140 yards (128 m)

medium fabric yarn in white with black dots, 20 yards (18.3 m)

stick shuttle, 12" (30.5 cm)

tapestry needle, 2½" (6.5 cm)

wooden comb or fork

scissors

Fig. 1

Fig. 2

1 Warp your large loom with the cotton rope in natural as you would your lap loom. It will accommodate a 4' x 6' (1.2 x 1.8 m) rug when woven all the way across the nail heads, but you can customize your size.

Start your first color block with the olive green fettuccia yarn. Weave 4 rows of plain weave and then reduce 2 warps on either side every 4 weft rows. This will create the same stair-step pattern used in other projects, but you'll use a diagonal interlock (pages 86–88) to make sure there isn't any pull between warp threads where the color blocks meet. Weave up for a total of 19 stair steps (Fig. 1).

As you work, be sure you continue arcing, bubbling, and gently batting down each weft row so you don't pull in the warp.

2 Flip your loom and weave the same shape with the same yarn on the opposite end (Fig. 2).

3 Your next section will be a shorter version of the same shape on top of the previous shape. Weave the light mint yarn all the way across your warp for 4 weft rows and then decrease 2 warps on each side for every 4 weft rows. When you need to cut another length of yarn, overlap your ends as shown and press them together with your weaving comb as you work that weft row down (Fig. 3). Create a total of 12 stair steps, or 48 weft rows of this color.

4 Flip your loom over again and repeat the same pattern (Fig. 4).

5 Add in your final color block for this first group of shapes with the ochre yarn. Above the light mint shape, weave all the way across for 4 weft rows. Decrease 2 warps for every 4 weft rows for a total of 5 stair steps and then increase 2 warps for every 4 weft rows (Fig. 5). This should meet up with the light mint area above it and create a reverse arrow shape on each end.

6 Next, fill in the negative spaces with a light pink color block. Thread the light pink yarn on the tapestry needle. Interlock your light pink yarn by stitching through the back side of the mint loop on the third warp as shown. Pull through until you have a 4" (10 cm) tail (Fig. 6).

7 Weave over the second warp and under the first warp (Fig. 7).

8 Weave in the opposite direction as usual and interlock again through the loop from the back side (Fig. 8). Stitching through the back side each time, no matter how the loop is angled, will create a more consistent design and a less bulky seam.

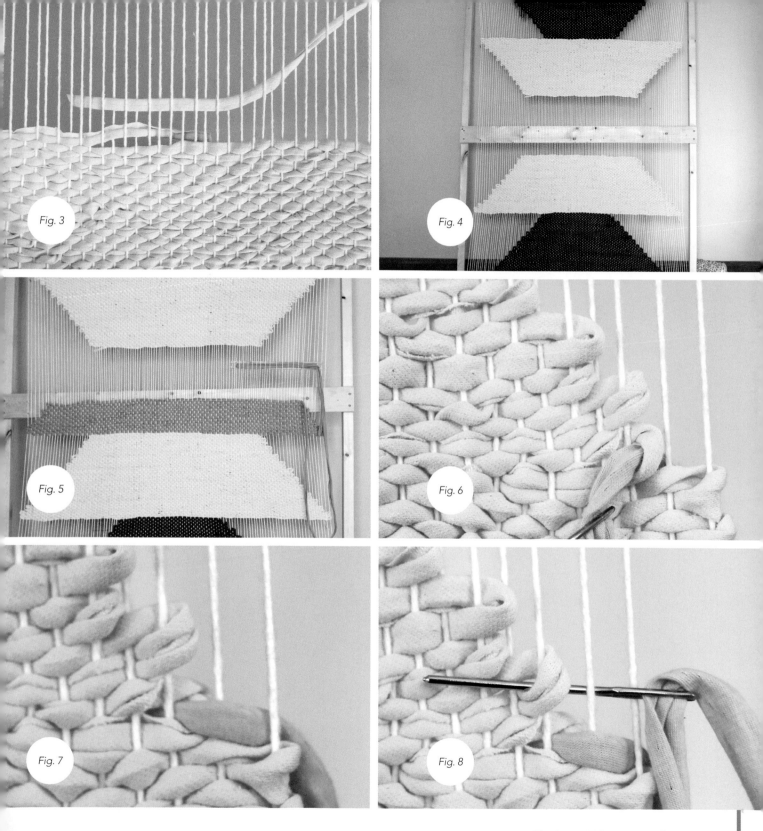

Fig. 3

Fig. 4

Fig. 5

Fig. 6

Fig. 7

Fig. 8

9 Weave back over those warps as you usually would and under the selvedge. Continue interlocking as you weave your way through this entire negative space next to the light mint yarn (Fig. 9).

Fig. 9

10 After you weave your last weft row in this negative space, weave back in about 5 warps to secure your tail and trim the end. This will leave a cleaner edge (Fig. 10).

11 Continue filling in your negative spaces until you are done with your rug. The olive green color block will share weft rows with the dark pink color block; the light mint color block will share weft rows with the light pink; and the ochre color block in the center of the rug will share weft rows with the white-and-black patterned color block. You don't have to weave them in a specific order as long as they all get filled in (Fig. 11).

Always be mindful that you aren't pulling too tightly as you weave. You may still end up with a slight curve toward the center of your weaving on a large project like this, but consider it one of those handmade imperfections that add charm.

Fig. 10

12 You shouldn't have any room left on either end of your loom, so carefully pull your warps off of your nail heads. I like to use my metal tapestry needle for this to save my fingers the wear and tear. Remove your warp from both outside edges toward the center to keep the warp and weft rows from pulling too much in one direction. Stitch in your tail ends along the edges of your rug.

Stand back and beam with pride!

Fig. 11

Weaving Terms

Arcing: The act of pulling your weft yarn through your warp upward and then downward to create an arc shape with your weft yarn. This is the step before bubbling and helps avoid an hourglass shape in your wall hanging caused by your weft yarn pulling too tightly against your warp threads.

Bubbling: The act of pressing your weft row down in sections to allow enough room to avoid pulling the selvedge ends toward each other. This can be done with your fingers or a tool and is followed by pushing the weft yarn down against the previous weft row with a weaving comb, fork, or fingers.

Color Block: One section of weaving in a specific color. It may reach all the way across the warp or just take up a portion of your design.

Decreasing: The act of weaving fewer warps on your next weft row.

Frame Loom: A solid shape with four sides that supports the warp and weft.

Increasing: The act of weaving additional warps on your next weft row.

Looping: Creating loops with your weft yarn over a round object in between warp threads. This provides a highly dimensional end result.

Rya Knot: Strands of yarn wrapped around two warp threads and pulled back through to the top to create a fringe or pile.

Selvedge: The outer warp thread on either side of your project.

Warp: The yarn that creates the foundation for your woven piece. It runs vertically over pegs or around a frame.

Weft: The yarn that is woven through the warp to create unique designs.

Glossary of Stitches

Plain Weave

The weft is woven over and under the warp in a consistent pattern. This is one of the most basic weaves for creating textiles, rugs, and wall art and is known for its strength and durability.

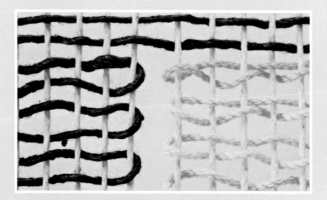

Straight Slit

A weaving technique that provides a strong vertical contrast between color blocks. It is usually used in small sections and densely packed because it can alter the structure of the weaving. It's used in kilim rugs and tapestries as well as wall art.

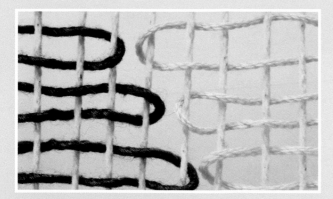

Diagonal Slit

A weaving technique that also provides a strong contrast between color blocks but is angled so that there is enough overlap between weft rows going in opposite directions that slits aren't noticeable, and the structure of the weaving isn't compromised. It's used in kilim rugs and tapestries as well as wall art.

Straight Interlock, Common Weft

A technique that joins two color blocks together by interlocking the weft rows but in between warp threads. The integrity of the structure is preserved, but it creates a little bit of a ridge in the pattern and doesn't have quite the same contrast between color blocks. It's commonly used when weaving functional textiles.

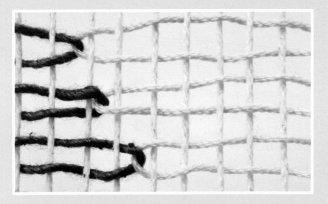

Diagonal Interlock, Common Weft

This technique also joins the weft rows in between warp threads but on the diagonal. It's more commonly used when weaving functional textiles.

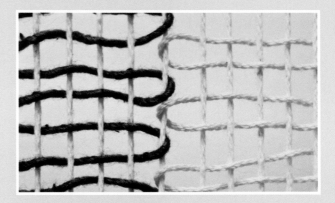

Straight Interlock, Common Warp

This technique also helps preserve the integrity of the structure by weaving around a shared warp thread, but this can create a little bit of bulk as well. It can create a slight dovetail-type design when tightly packed. It's commonly used when working with thinner fibers and when weaving functional textiles.

Diagonal Interlock, Common Warp

This technique is another way to maintain the integrity of the structure, but it can lose the strong contrast between color blocks. It is similar to the straight interlock, common warp in that it creates a slight dovetail-type pattern when densely packed. It's commonly used when working with thinner fibers and when weaving functional textiles.

Soumak

This is a stitch that creates loops around warps using the weft yarn. The most basic soumak stitch wraps over the top of two warp threads in one direction and then under one warp thread in the opposite direction before repeating. Variations include multiple warp threads forward and backward, such as four forward and two backward. Two weft rows of soumak stitched in opposite directions create a herringbone or braided pattern (not shown here). In the image, the top example is a basic soumak, the second example is a variation with more warps being included in each stitch, and the third example is a basic soumak with wool roving.

Resources

Premade Looms and Loom Kits

Black Sheep Goods
blacksheepgoods615.etsy.com

Fünem Studio
funemstudio.etsy.com

Loom & Spindle
loomandspindleau.etsy.com

Meghan Bogden Shimek
meghanshimek.com

Oake & Ashe
oakeandashe.etsy.com

Roving Handmade Textiles
rovingtextiles.etsy.com

The Unusual Pear
theunusualpear.etsy.com

Wild Columbine Textile
wildcolumbinetextile.etsy.com

Wood Creek Looms
woodcreeklooms.etsy.com

Fiber Sources

Bernat
yarnspirations.com

Berroco
berroco.com

Cascade Yarns
cascadeyarns.com

The Fibre Co.
thefibreco.com

Ganxxet
ganxxet.com

Habu Textiles
habutextiles.com

Hand Made Modern
target.com

Hedgehog Fibres
shop.hedgehogfibres.com

I Love This Cotton! Yarn
hobbylobby.com

Knit Collage
knitcollage.com

Knit Stitch Yarn
knitstitchyarn.etsy.com

Koigu Wool Designs
koigu.com

Lily Sugar 'n Cream
sugarncream.com

Lion Brand Yarn
lionbrand.com

Madelinetosh
madelinetosh.com

Malabrigo
malabrigoyarn.com

Manos del Uruguay
manosyarns.com

Mohair & More
mohairandmore.etsy.com

O Wool
o-wool.com

Old Homestead Alpacas
oldhomesteadalpacas.etsy.com

Purl Soho
purlsoho.com

Quince & Co.
quinceandco.com

Republic of Wool
republicofwool.com

Sauked In Farm
saukedinfarm.etsy.com

Spud & Chloe
spudandchloe.com

Ugly Hank
uglyhank.etsy.com

Woodland Trail Farm
woodlandtrailfarm.etsy.com

Yarns Used in Projects

The following are the specific yarns I used to make the projects in this book.

I Want Candy, Wall Hanging, page 34

Lily Sugar 'n Cream (100% cotton, 120 yd/71 g), Hot Orange

Lily Sugar 'n Cream (100% cotton, 200 yd/113 g), Rose Pink

Lily Sugar 'n Cream (100% cotton, 120 yd/71 g), Tangerine

Lily Sugar 'n Cream (100% cotton, 706 yd/400 g), Soft Ecru

Both Ways Wall Hanging, page 44

Bernat Roving (80% acrylic/20% wool, 120 yd/100 g), Low Tide

Woodland Trail Farm Alpaca (100% alpaca, 90 yd/85 g), Minty Green

The Fibre Co. Knightsbridge (65% baby llama/25% merino wool/10% silk, 120 yd/50 g), Poole

Purl Soho Super Soft Merino Wool (100% merino wool, 87 yd/100 g), Ochre Yellow

Manos del Uruguay Clasica Wool (100% wool, 138 yd/100 g), #2060 80 Highlighter

Lily Sugar 'n Cream (100% cotton, 100 yd/71 g), Soft Ecru

Vintage dark green cotton yarn

Opal Wall Hanging, page 56

Lily Sugar 'n Cream (100% cotton, 706 yd/400 g), Soft Ecru

Quince & Co. Chickadee Wool (100% wool, 181 yd/50 g), Honey

Manos del Uruguay Maxima Wool (100% extrafine merino wool, 219 yd/100 g), Zinnia

Spud & Chloe Superwash (55% wool/45% organic cotton, 160 yd/100 g), Watermelon

Lily Sugar'n Cream (100% cotton, 120 yd/70 g), Seabreeze

Vintage cream wool yarn

Group Hug Wall Hanging, page 64

Lily Sugar 'n Cream (100% cotton, 706 yd/400 g), Soft Ecru

Mohair & More Wool Roving (100% merino wool, 226 g), Undyed

Woodland Trail Farm Alpaca (100% alpaca, 90 yd/85 g), Minty Green

The Fibre Co. Acadia (60% merino wool/20% baby alpaca/20% silk, 145 yd/50 g), Amber

Vintage cream wool yarn

Band Wife Wall Hanging, page 72

Lily Sugar 'n Cream (100% cotton, 706 yd/400 g), Soft Ecru

Quince & Co. Puffin (100% wool, 112 yd/100 g) Peacock

The Fiber Co. Knightsbridge (65% baby llama/25% merino wool/10% silk, 120 yd/50 g), Grasmere

Quince & Co. Kestrel (100% organic linen, 76 yd/50 g), Aegean

The Fibre Co. Knightsbridge (65% baby llama/25% merino wool/10% silk, 120 yd/50 g), Poole

Lily Sugar'n Cream (100% cotton, 120 yd/70 g), Seabreeze

Woodland Trail Farm Alpaca (100% alpaca, 90 yd/85 g), Minty Green

Vintage cream wool yarn

The Stars at Night Wall Hanging, page 78

Lily Sugar 'n Cream (100% cotton, 706 yd/400 g), Soft Ecru

Woodland Trail Farm Alpaca (100% alpaca, 90 yd/85 g), Minty Green

The Fibre Co. Acadia (60% merino wool/20% baby alpaca/20% silk, 145 yd/50 g), Amber

Quince & Co. Finch (100% wool, 221 yd/50 g), Marsh Green

Quince & Co. Piper (50% superfine Texas merino wool/50% super kid Texas mohair, 305 yd/50 g), San Angelo

Purl Soho Super Soft Merino Wool (100% merino wool, 87 yd/100 g), Ochre Yellow

Lily Sugar 'n Cream (100% cotton, 120 yd/71 g), Coral

Hand Made Modern (100% wool, 3 yd/7 g), Cranberry

Old Homestead Alpacas Roving (100% alpaca, 7 g), Natural

Vintage off-white wool yarn

Poesy Wall Hanging, page 90

Lily Sugar 'n Cream (100% cotton, 706 yd/400 g), Soft Ecru

Purl Soho Super Soft Merino (100% merino wool, 87 yd/100 g), Grapefruit

Purl Soho Super Soft Merino (100% merino wool, 87 yd/100 g), Ballet Pink

Purl Soho Super Soft Merino (100% merino wool, 87 yd/100 g), Ochre Yellow

Purl Soho Super Soft Merino (100% merino wool, 87 yd/100 g), Sea Salt

Quince & Co. Piper Wool (50% superfine Texas merino wool/50%

super kid Texas mohair, 305 yd/50 g), San Angelo

Ugly Hank (100% wool, 20 yd), Madder

Triple Scoop Wall Hanging, page 100

Lily Sugar 'n Cream (100% cotton, 706 yd/400 g), Soft Ecru

The Fibre Co. Acadia (60% merino wool/20% baby alpaca/20% silk, 145 yd/50 g), Amber

Purl Soho Mulberry Merino (80% extrafine merino wool/20% mulberry silk, 247 yd/100 g), Ochre Yellow

Koigu Merino Crepe (100% merino wool, 114 yd/50 g), K-1532

Koigu Merino Crepe (100% merino wool, 114 yd/50 g), K-1533

I Love This Cotton! (100% cotton, 180 yd/99 g), Mango

Vintage peach yarn

Flighty Wall Hanging, page 108

Purl Soho Habu Oak Cotton Gima (100% cotton, 109 yd/28.5 g), N-100

Mohair & More Roving (100% wool, 6 yd/113 g), Mint

Malabrigo (100% merino wool, 100 yd/100 g), Tuareg

Milkmaid Braid Hanging, page 114

Tandy dyed cowhide

Manos del Uruguay Maxima Wool (100% extrafine merino wool, 219 yd/100 g), Zinnia

The Fibre Co. Terra (40% baby alpaca/40% wool/20% silk, 98 yd/50 g), Redwood

Mohair & More Roving (100% wool, 6 yd/113 g), Mint

Lily Sugar 'n Cream (100% cotton, 706 yd/400 g), Soft Ecru

Cascade Superwash (100% superwash merino wool, 136 yd/50 g), Coral

Take Me Somewhere Clutch, page 124

Lily Sugar 'n Cream (100% cotton, 706 yd/400 g), Soft Ecru

Ganxxet Fabric Yarn (cotton/elastane, 160 yd/907 g), Mustard

Ganxxet Fabric Yarn (cotton/elastane, 65 yd/567 g), white-and-black print

Ganxxet Fabric Yarn (cotton/elastane, 160 yd/907 g), Nassau

Indigo Dreams Table Runner, page 134

Lily Sugar 'n Cream (100% cotton, 706 yd/400 g), Soft Ecru

Knit Stitch Superwash (100% merino wool, 220 yd/100 g), Indigo

Lion Brand Wool-Ease (80% acrylic, 20% wool, 153 yd/142 g), Fisherman

Fringe Benefits Pillow Sham, page 140

Berroco Maya (85% pima cotton/15% baby alpaca, 137 yd/50 g), Sombra

Knit Collage Sister (100% wool, 100 yd/215 g), Camel Heather

Lion Brand Wool-Ease (80% acrylic, 20% wool, 153 yd/142 g), Fisherman

Purl Soho Mulberry Merino (80% extrafine merino wool/20% mulberry silk, 247 yd/100 g), Ochre Yellow

Ugly Hank (100% wool, 20 yd), Osage Orange Sawdust

Last Summer Statement Wall Hanging, page 148

Lily Sugar 'n Cream (100% cotton, 706 yd/400 g), Soft Ecru

Mohair & More Roving (100% wool, 6 yd/113 g), Natural

Lion Brand Wool-Ease (80% acrylic, 20% wool, 153 yd/142 g), Fisherman

Quince & Co. Puffin (100% American wool, 112 yd/100 g), Peacock

Koigu Merino Crepe (100% merino wool, 114 yd/50 g), K-1111

Knit Collage Sister (100% wool, 100 yd/215 g), Camel Heather

Knit Collage Cast Away (99% wool, 1% polyester, 70 yd/100 g), Pink Cactus

Purl Soho Habu Oak Cotton Gima (100% cotton, 109 yd/28.5 g), N-100

The Fibre Co. Terra (40% baby alpaca/40% wool/20% silk, 98 yd/50 g), Black Locust Bark

Habu Textiles Dyed Linen (100% linen, 300 yd/50 g), XS-55

Vintage off-white polyester yarn

Vintage off-white wool yarn

Positive Vibes Rug, page 160

Lily Sugar 'n Cream (100% cotton, 706 yd/400 g), Soft Ecru

Ganxxet Fettucia Yarn (100% polyester, 140 yd/340 g), Green

Ganxxet Fabric Yarn (cotton/elastane blend, 140 yd/907 g), Fresno

Ganxxet Fabric Yarn (cotton/elastane blend, 160 yd/907 g), Cannes

Ganxxet Fabric Yarn (cotton/elastane blend, 140 yd/907 g), Nassau

Ganxxet Fabric Yarn (cotton/elastane, 160 yd/907 g), Mustard

Ganxxet Fabric Yarn (cotton/elastane, 65 yd/567 g), white-and-black print

Index

fw

a content + ecommerce company

20 19 18 17 16   5 4 3 2 1

Distributed in Canada by Fraser Direct
100 Armstrong Avenue
Georgetown, ON, Canada L7G 5S4
Tel: (905) 877-4411

Distributed in the U.K. and Europe by F&W MEDIA INTERNATIONAL
Brunel House, Newton Abbot, Devon, TQ12 4PU, England
Tel: (+44) 1626 323200, Fax: (+44) 1626 323319
E-mail: enquiries@fwmedia.com

SRN: 16WV03
ISBN-13: 978-1-63250-431-9

PDF SRN: EP13255
PDF ISBN-13: 978-1-63250-432-6

ePub SRN: EP13226
ePub ISBN-13: 978-1-63250-433-3

Edited by Christine Doyle
Designed by Nicola DosSantos
Photography by Rachel Denbow and Janae Hardy

Metric Conversion Chart

To Convert	To	Multiply By
Inches	Centimeters	2.54
Centimeters	Inches	0.4
Feet	Centimeters	30.5
Centimeters	Feet	0.03
Yards	Meters	0.9
Meters	Yards	1.1

About the Author

Rachel Denbow is a self-taught weaver with a strong urge to create on a daily basis. She has been sharing how to sew, decorate, build, art journal, and parent with creativity for over ten years through her blog *Smile and Wave* (smileandwavediy.com). She is a regular DIY contributor to *A Beautiful Mess* blog and has authored over a dozen creative e-courses in the last seven years. She enjoys experimenting with new techniques and encouraging other creatives to make time to make things.

Acknowledgments

I want to thank my family for always supporting and encouraging my creativity. Grandmother, thanks for buying me that bead-loom kit for Christmas when I was younger. Meemaw, thanks for letting me raid your vintage fabric stash. Dad, thanks for knowing about the maker community. Joe, thanks for letting me dress you up in my tutu so we could perform the Nutcracker ballet. Mom, thanks for passing down the creative genes and being the first person I wanted to call to share the exciting news that this book was happening.

To two of my dearest friends, Elsie Larson and Emma Chapman, who always inspire me to dream big dreams and have offered me a platform for doing what I love most—teaching people to make all the things. You both always talked about *when* I'd write a book and not *if* I'd write a book. Your confidence in me is such a special thing. To Alison Faulkner, who gave me my first opportunity to teach a weaving class while also teaching everyone to be awesome.

To so many other creative friends who regularly challenge me to do my best by putting out their own excellent work as they share their gifts: Katie Shelton, Elise Cripe, Rubyellen Bratcher, Laura Gummerman, Ashley Campbell, Sarah Rhodes, Mandi Johnson, Ruthie Covert. I'm so lucky to call you friends.

To the talented weaving women who design from well-developed viewpoints while continuing to push their own creative boundaries: Maryanne Moodie, Janelle Pietrzak, Meghan Shimek, Kelly Neistat, Natalie Miller, Erin Barrett, Sarah Neubert, and so many others. Your own work inspires many and is such a gift. Your encouragement of a positive and ever-growing weaving community will forever have ripple effects.

To the crafting community at large for validating my need to make my own things and telling me it's normal to have this many craft supplies.

To my editors for their help in getting the best version of this book on the shelves, my agent for being just as enthusiastic at my second attempt to write a book, and to my friend and photographer Janae Hardy for lending her magic and being such a joy to work with.

I need to thank my sweet children, who have taught me how strong I am.

Lastly, I want to thank my husband, Brett, for always believing this was possible and for picking up all of the slack on the domestic and parenting duties so I could meet my big deadline. I couldn't have done this without your love and support.

Continue to weave new skills into your art with these fantastic resources from Interweave

Weaving Made Easy: Revised and Updated

17 Projects Using a Rigid-Heddle Loom

Liz Gipson

9781620336809 | $24.99

Next Steps in Weaving

What You Never Knew You Needed to Know

Pattie Graver

9781620336274 | $27.99

The Weaver's Inkle Dictionary

400 Warp-Faced Weaves

Anne Dixon

9781596686472 | $29.99

Available at your favorite retailer or WEAVINGTODAY.COM

WEAVING TODAY

Weaving Today is the town square for handweavers and the online community for *Handwoven* magazine. Get weaving techniques, instruction, and trends in free weaving blogs, as well as eBooks, media galleries, and more! WEAVINGTODAY.COM

HANDWOVEN

Handwoven is the premiere resource for everyone interested in weaving, from beginners to seasoned professionals. Each issue introduces you to weavers from around the world and is filled with tips and tricks of the trade and the latest tools. Plus you'll be among the first to know about new innovations or creative ideas. HANDWOVENMAGAZINE.COM